The Salvation Equation

Changing the World
One Divine Potential at a Time

Dedicated to family, friends, colleagues and every individual who has aspired to understand the greater possibilities of the human condition.

<u>The Salvation Equation: Changing the World One Divine Potential at a Time</u>

By David M. Rogers

Foreword

1. Introduction: Overview

    A. Need for a Unifying Framework

    B. The Underlying Moral Imperative.

    C. Change by Degrees

    D.   The Five Foundational Statements of Potential

    Epilogue: The two Possible Competing Models of the Universe

2. Seven Basic Assumptions Needed to Identify your Divine Nature and Potential

    A. A Higher Power or Being Exists, traditionally known as "God".

    B. You cannot assume to Restrict God's Operations or Abilities Based on your own Experiences or Perceptions.

    E. God Loves you and cares about your ultimate potential; you have been placed in a position to act freely upon that divine potential.

    D. God's characteristics are predictable, consistent and knowable as you need them; He knows you and you can progressively learn of His divine nature.

    E. You are able to possess a portion of divine characteristics.

    F. You may always be empowered, from within and without, as you reach for your highest potentials.

G. You will be held accountable for the achievement of your ultimate potential.

Epilogue: Two Orders of Mind

3. Overview of The Salvation Equation

A. The Equation metaphor.

B. The direction and slope; Positive and Negative Potentials:

A Four Point Test of Principle and Application

C. Chance versus created opportunity.

D. The cost of inaction.

E. We can always change our slope

Epilogue: Universal Mathematical language

4. A Three Part Model of a Human Being and the Key Potentials Within

A. Potentials of Spirit

B. Potentials of Mind

C. Potentials of Body

Epilogue: The Laws of conservation of Energy and Matter

5. The Fundamental Necessity of Faith in Your Own Ultimate Potential.

Epilogue: The why and how of personal perspective.

6. We Are Always Thinking, Choosing and Becoming…Something.

    A. The process of becoming is a permanent part of our nature.

    B. Three progressive life phases and orientations of becoming, perspective and self.

    Epilogue: The Religious Metaphor of the Great Cliff

7. Six Basic Assumptions Associated with Divine Human Potential.

    A. You are more than the sum of our biological parts and processes.

    B. Intelligence and Will are capable of expansion and increase.

    C. You must apply the process of becoming; Law of the Harvest.

    D. You are constantly required to exercise will.

    E. You can always change the direction and slope of potential fulfillment.

    F. Your existence is best seen as a chapter in a larger work.

    Epilogue: A Universal Database?

8. The Six Levels of Comprehending and Internalizing Your Potential.

    A. Blind acceptance from another source.

    B. Forming behaviors and attitudes to avoid punishment.

    C. Forming behaviors and attitudes to obtain a reward.

    D. Seeing potential as a beneficial choice.

    E. Seeing potential as the highest virtue.

    F. Internalizing and becoming our potential.

    Epilogue: An Inconvenient continuum

<u>Foreword</u>

"All great acts of genius began with the same consideration: do not be constrained by your present reality". – Leonardo Da Vinci

It is a fact that each one of us learns from birth to form assumptions to understand and define the world around us. Most of those assumptions are either learned through tradition, education or social networks. But some of the assumptions are innate. They seem to be "pre-programmed". Perhaps you can identify some of those "natural" and intuitive ways you tend to see the world around you. They are not provable to anyone but yourself, yet you seem to know them. They are your own personal truth. Each one of us has a built in desire to discover meaning. What may not be often recognized are the assumptions behind how we look for and define that meaning.

The great diversity of world culture, religion and politics that has been thrown into a common mix in a relatively short period of decades leads to both cross fertilization of ideas and anxiety of difference. Also, as science and a bent towards humanistic culture gradually overwrite more long-standing tradition, the whisper of the divine nature of man that has been incumbent for centuries seems to fade into less and less significance. The deafening demands of modern science push spirituality into the corner of quaint but seemingly irrelevant tradition. But is the possibility of divinity in each and every one of us really insignificant?

That may be the most important assumption you, or anyone for that matter, may ever choose to explore or live by. Is your nature partly divine? Does it matter? And if you were to choose to live according to the premise of an attachment to a divinity greater than yourself, what would your thoughts and decisions look like? Would it change anything? How would your personal priorities change if you operated under the assumptions of continuing and divine existence? How would your concept of self-worth and importance of thought and action be transformed?

The Salvation Equation attempts to address these important questions based on a common language that can cross the barriers of culture, religion or politics. This book seeks to have a personal conversation with you, as if we were sitting down to a long meal together. It is a discussion, a heart to heart regarding how certain assumptions help you view the world and how that has an effect upon you and your perceptions of meaning.

When you break each thought and action down on principle as it applies to your own innate potential, you can develop a language or method of seeing such assumptions for what they are. And what they might mean to you. And you can develop desires to sort, activate, prioritize and recognize your potentials for what they imply based on certain sets of assumptions.

As Leonardo DaVinci points out, the assumptions through which we view the world can change over time and with experience. How much more completely might you be equipped to live life to its fullest if you can recognize those potentials for their natural use and benefit, both for yourself and others? What sort of world might we have if each one of us learned to recognize not just the basic potentials we possess, but could, through the development of potentials of a more lasting or divine nature, reach for the highest levels of our innate self and discover new and broader meaning and purpose? What sort of culture might we ultimately surround ourselves with if everyone sought for the highest aspects of self and exercised them daily? Would the very priorities of our society change? Would this tumultuous world become a more peaceful and cooperative place?

No matter what you might currently think of the nature of the human soul, it is fruitful to examine the assumptions that help identify the spirit or soul, that part of intelligence and will that would have an ability to exist beyond physical constraints, as a continuing entity, with the implications thereof, and the corollaries that oppose such assumptions. With those ideas in mind, I hope you enjoy the information and thoughts put forth in the Salvation Equation.

Chapter 1

Introduction and Overview

<u>The Need for a Unifying Framework</u>:

If you could evaluate the lives of the most successful people in history, you would likely find a trend universal among all of them. They would be spectacular at a few things, understand a little about a great many things, and be blithely ignorant of everything else. But one universal truth applies to every one of history's greats, as it applies to each one of us. There is no definable limit to human potential. No mortal person could possibly fulfill all of their ultimate potential in the short span of a lifetime. The absolute pinnacle of that potential is simply too expansive. Yet this does not prevent the concept of "a life well lived" to encompass reaching for that potential in every positive way possible. Indeed, if we are to ascribe and understand real purpose to our lives, the absolutes of human potential are as valuable a reference point as any.

If there is one additional fact almost everyone can agree upon it is that we are living in a world that is changing rapidly. We are in many ways truly immersed in the information age. General information, science, technology, sociology, psychology and so many related fields are multiplying new deposits to our library of human knowledge at an ever increasing rate. Local economies that became national economies are now becoming global economies with their requisite exchange of information, technologies, methods and ideas. Yet among all of the information available today, the question must be asked: throughout the proliferation of all of this information has mankind been able to maintain a clear definition of the true nature and potential of each individual? Have we multiplied both the secular and the divine possibilities inherent in each of us?

Or has the amount of new and increasing information available blurred that vision and created confusion regarding the common touch points that describe the innermost human potentials? In your own journey of education, experience and understanding has modern science and the increasing influence of secular and humanist philosophies convinced you that you are only the sum of your biological and behavioral parts? For millennia many visionary savants have often felt we are more than this. Whether guided by philosophy, religion or simple superstition they have envisioned themselves as part human and part something else, something more, something divine.

The focus of secularism and the specific pursuits given priority under its tenets have a useful role. If your goal is to be an engineer, it is wise focus on the things that will make you the most informed and best engineer you can be. The same ethic should apply no matter your chosen pursuits, whether you enjoy nursing, acting, education or auto mechanics. The Salvation Equation is about priorities, not about common technical specifics. The day will come in every life when secular pursuits and priorities fade and we are each left to stare into the nearing gateway of the eternities. In that day it will become obvious that the most important pursuits involve forging knowledge and character that has the opportunity to survive, assuming there is a next chapter to existence. Will the sum total of a life be all of the secular knowledge we might obtain? Or is there something broader and deeper that needs to be given priority? In other words, is it more important to spend the bulk of our lives pursuing skills and knowledge that will not transfer to our broader eternal nature, or will we prioritize those potentials that may survive with us indefinitely?

Are you, as a thinking and rational individual, clear on such priorities and the principles that guide and define all aspects of your nature? Or are you losing touch, having your intuitive and sometimes indescribably divine character scrubbed away in the ever imposing body of academic theory and research as defined by secularism in our modern world? What must you know and understand in order to keep the fullest picture of the complex being that you are in focus?

Information proliferates, science progresses and yet there is still a lack of agreement on the deepest nature or the most significant commonalities of human experience. Because science and technology have progressed so rapidly and become so commonplace in our educational disciplines, they have begun to replace some of the more traditional and spiritual frameworks through which we have long viewed ourselves. And it is the more coldly scientific voices that are dominating modern discussion, permeating our institutions of higher learning. These voices seek to disqualify any hint of divinity or any thought or order beyond the empirical bounds of science, as described by the latest academics du jour, from any discussion of our nature. Yet despite all of its searching, science alone has never been able to provide the definitive answers to such urgent questions regarding the human condition. Science evolves, but what of those human traits and potentials that have always remained constant throughout time?

Rather than write your spiritual or intuitive natures out of the picture, is it not best to explore both aspects of your life with similar zeal and fortitude? How can you establish a means of speaking a common language, as science seeks to do in all of its endeavors, in the intuitive and spiritual parts of your life? Despite the many philosophies, religions and traditions that have attempted to set parameters and clarify spiritual or divine nature, how might we all come to a common language that can describe those feelings and impressions that are found universally in almost any spiritual or holistic line of thought or tradition?

In many ways the world is shrinking. Many countries that were once exotic or mysterious, with their varied historical perspectives, are joining in a mainstream exchange of commerce, culture and ideas. Even within a native country, the various subcultures, traditions and political or religious facets of an individual's life are overlapping more frequently with this open availability of modern information. What we inevitably discover in this increasing maelstrom of information and ideas is that ultimately people are people and we have certain things in common that are not necessarily specifically taught by our culture, education, religious upbringing (or lack thereof) or political inclinations. These commonalities run deep within us all. We all have certain potentials in common, physical, mental and spiritual in nature. These potentials can become a shared language that allow us all to be bound together in a brotherhood and sisterhood that extends beyond political or cultural borders. You have an opportunity to look at others through similar, common lenses when you consider the numerous potentials that we all share.

In the final analysis, it does not matter as much as you might have once thought that you may be distinguished by politics, education, cultural tendencies or different languages. Inwardly, you possess certain fundamental characteristics that define a human being; concepts of humanity we all share in common. While it is true that the perceptions and interpretations of self may be shaded by the social, political, religious or cultural traditions endemic to your native environment, the foundations and fundamental principles that lead you towards your ultimate potential remain universal and unchangeable from person to person, culture to culture and nation to nation. These foundations rest in the physical and measurable world in which you live and in the metaphysical, intuitive and divine world which may be also ever present.

There exists an increasing influence of the theories of empirical science, humanism, or more recently the tenets of Cultural Marxism, marching through and dominating many western institutions of influence and thought. These mindsets seek to define a human being only in terms of their physical nature or in terms of their ability to contribute to hard science, economic, social, political or labor initiatives. The Salvation Equation posits that if an individual is ever to reach their highest potentials, we must assume that we are more than the sum of our physical abilities, perceptions, reason or perceived value to societal norms. We must clearly recognize that there is a specific commonality that all people share, and that is the spark and essence of the divine within each one of us that extends beyond the realms of science and into the realm of our own spirituality and eternal nature. Indeed, it is this tenuous but critical balance between the intuitive or spiritual and secular, or rational, which has underpinned the rise and achievements of the modern world.

You must view yourself as more than the sum of biological parts and your physical experiences. If you are ever to achieve your absolute best, you must clearly view yourself as an expansive intelligence that can progress from within and without, and that a significant part of who you are originates from beyond the merely physical. In other words, you must learn from science all that empirical research and methodology offers within its appropriate applications, but you must not discount the intuitive and ultimately divine aspects of your nature if you are to create a complete and common understanding of yourself and apply it to your highest ultimate potentials.

Modern science and the empirical mandate it carries forward should not have the absolute last word in the description of a human being or human experience. While most empirical study is noteworthy and usually beneficial, to assume that cold hard science or the philosophies of Humanism hold the final answers and outline the uttermost boundaries of your existence is to risk missing an important dimension of who you ultimately are and may become.

Rational thought based primarily on observable experience has a place and use within modern deliberation. But while the empiricist says "show me the evidence and I will believe it," our intuitive natures suggest the mindset should be reversed. The inquiry into our more divine potentials should be stated as "show me the evidence that it does not exist and I shall disregard it, for somehow in those quiet and profound moments I seem to tangibly sense and understand it." Mere discussion or argument is ineffective as sophistry from either point of view is only carried by the person that can argue more technically or effectively a on a particular subject. And argument may never settle the issue between the debating parties. If you are to truly explore the divine potentials you carry, time and experience are the only final answer to the test of their true existence.

The problem with the divine aspects of a human being, at least from a scientific or humanist point of view, is that your deepest and most profound thoughts, feelings and aspirations and the internal progress they bring to you simply are not empirically measurable. You come to know them, they become real to you, and you can often quantify them and make sense of them within the world in which you live. They may be consistently repeatable, but you cannot often describe them in measurable terms to others. You can consistently experience them and you can get dependable and repeatable results for yourself within your own point of view. But those results are yours and yours alone. They are not transferable to others. Only your outward behaviors can be measured in any significant way, and that often not to a level that comprehends the experiences behind them.

Yet they make up the most important and dearest sense of who you feel you are. Love, for example, is not measurable, and the most intricate measurements of hormonal levels, change in heart rate, skin temperature change and pupil dilation will not come close to describing all that occurs when love passes between two people. You can imagine and have dreams and ambitions, but no measurement of electrical brain activity can summarize the process of turning an imagined idea or dream into reality. The depth of such experience, as real as it is to our experience, is beyond any consistent measurement based on current science.

You should never ignore or downplay the importance of hard science and the new frontiers, products and innovations that research and progressive applied scientific theory yield. But you must also never ignore nor discount the more internal and immeasurable potentials you possess. You must assume they exist simply by the fact that they are common experiences that can be shared by anyone who is attuned to their inner conscience. The fact that the thoughts, ideas, feelings, aspirations and physical activity that surround your daily labors to become the best of whatever you envision yourself to be cannot always be viewed or measured by others is not a justifiable reason to deny their importance to your overall development. Your wholeness, your completeness as an individual, depends on those immeasurable nuances.

The Salvation Equation maintains that there are certain innate principles and dynamics of both human and divine origin that guide and define all human existence. These principles are a bridge between the physical world in which you live and a larger spiritual reality we must all eventually embrace. The Salvation Equation attempts to help you comprehend these principles and dynamics in a language that can easily translate across cultural, political or socio-economic lines. It allows you to expand your thinking about who you are and what you can become either within or beyond traditional categorizations or identifiers. It establishes a foundation of principles that allow you to grow, expand and prosper in whatever positive direction or endeavor you should choose to pursue.

It also states that these principles and dynamics are ultimate guidelines that affect the processes that maximize your potential regardless of your personal background or experiences. They can be universally applied in any context. While these principles do not attempt to supersede science, they do eventually need to be given appropriate and equal footing as credible aspects of human existence and experience despite their present subjectivity. To achieve your utmost, you must assume that you are governed in your development by the hard and measureable empirical parameters as well as by intuitive, spiritual and often unseen dynamics. Envision yourself as an interesting combination of the material and the divine. You must consider, understand and embrace both aspects of your nature to give yourself a complete picture.

It seems to be human nature to try to organize and classify ourselves and others into convenient "boxes" and categories. You are generally inundated from your earliest age with cues and suggestions of who you are and what is expected to be important. Many of these messages are clothed in the language, traditions and expectations of your native culture, family structure, religion, social class, educational systems and political systems. In some parts of the world, these cues and impressions have been passed down for centuries. In other parts of the world, change is so rapid that past cultural cues are rapidly morphing, being transformed and replaced by more modern interpretations. However you come by them, you often find it easier to relate to the world around you by creating these limited classifications. You might be tempted to label someone as "funny," "grumpy," "smart," "stupid," "liberal," "conservative," "crass," "cultured," "obnoxious," "sensitive", "endearing," "intellectual," "uneducated," "spiritual," "materialistic" or any number of convenient categorizations.

The Salvation Equation suggests that you should, through the understanding of your common potentials, transcend such categorization. Such labels are created to more easily make sense of the world and to more easily attempt to understand other individuals. The main pitfall of such a mindset is that it may remove the responsibility of working through the process of understanding each other beyond such manufactured categories; once you have placed someone into a "box," you often relieve yourself of the difficulties of developing a deeper perspective of that individual. It also inhibits your ability develop your own potentials beyond those perceived expectations of such categories. Many of your life experiences will not conveniently fit into simplified categories. You are a complex entity in a complex world and require time, experience, work and considerable thought and contemplation to effectively realize your own potentials and relate fully to the potentials of others.

In light of this, the Salvation Equation is offered as a framework that can help you understand that you have certain, common, unchanging potentials. It is intended to give you ways to think of yourself and your ultimate potential in a common language that can transcend man-made boundaries. Even in this era of widespread information, there remains the tendency to try to separate or categorize yourself and others based on political, religious or cultural guidelines. While celebrating a diversity of ideas and perspectives is an enriching process, it is this book's intention to identify and form ideas and perspectives that have the capacity to unite in the most basic common foundations of humanity notwithstanding an immense range of diversity. It is intended to equip you with a common model that allows you to tangibly look within and understand your important potentials and the breadth of their nature and effect.

Potentials are discussed from the perspective of both the human and the divine. Human potentials are those that primarily aid you in growing, learning and becoming successful in the activities that pertain directly to the basic functions of your life. They address what you need to live, grow and prosper throughout your given mortal years and understand and function within the temporal environment around you. Your divine potentials encompass all of the aspects of your human potentials but also prepare you for a more extensive learning process that reaches beyond the obvious necessities of daily life. Your divine potentials encompass those characteristics you must assume would remain intact beyond your mortal existence, such as acquired knowledge and the discipline of your emotions and intellectual processes. In a sense, all of your potentials carry a hint of the divine. Some are simply more directly applicable to the idea of an expanding and eternal nature than others.

Perhaps the first question you might ask is: "Is this a religious book?" While it will directly promote fundamental assumptions of your divine and eternal nature and outline reasons for considering the existence of and your connection to God or a Supreme Power or Being, the Salvation Equation is not intended to establish or promote any particular set of religious tenets or doctrines. It is designed to identify those common and fundamental aspects of human experience and your ultimate potentials that are found in almost any concept of faith or any subscription to a religious system of beliefs that revolve around the adoration of a Supreme Being or higher power. The Salvation Equation also does not endorse any political idea or system per se, but is designed to promote the establishment of a common commitment to your individual potential that can be translated to a local, community, national or global perspective.

The Salvation Equation is intended to establish and clarify a set of underlying principles and assumptions that can be applied to any individual regardless of their background. It seeks to establish a common language that allows you to freely understand and discuss the most important commonalities that you share as a human being across established political and religious lines. The Salvation Equation is designed to emphasize all the innate and learned characteristics you share regardless of your affiliations so that each individual may relate their potentials with another in a spirit of mutual understanding. How you might choose to apply the principles contained within this book in terms of the traditions, tenets, creeds, vows, sacraments, ordinances or covenants of a particular religion or set of beliefs is up to you. The principles behind the Salvation Equation are not unique to any specific set of beliefs, but may find commonality in almost all concepts of faith.

The Salvation Equation is put forward to equip you with a common way of thinking about yourself that others can equally understand and internalize, allowing you to communicate a common foundation upon which you can effectively realize your highest potentials, both human and divine. You can use this perspective to look at any other person with the understanding that they intrinsically share with you in all of the principles and aspects that the Salvation Equation suggests. This creates not only a powerful self-perspective, but a powerful bond between individuals at any level. While the internalization of a personal principle is almost entirely an intuitive process, you can experiment with these principles by applying them consistently in your daily activities. If the ideas and principles in this book are internalized, exercised and applied consistently, you will see progress and growth in your own potential. You will also realize an enhanced understanding of other people and their life experiences. It provides a focused lens through which you may evaluate and envision your highest potentials and the potentials of others.

Another question that might be asked is: "Is this a how-to book?" The answer to this is not specifically as the genre currently exists. There are a plethora of how-to, self-help and motivational works available. A few examples would include "Seven Habits of Highly Effective People" by Dr. Stephen R. Covey, "Think and Grow Rich" by Napoleon Hill, "The Success Principles" by Jack Canfield, "How the Best Leaders Lead" by Brian Tracy, "Rich Dad Poor Dad" by Robert T. Kiyosaki, "Awaken the Giant Within" by Tony Robbins, "Think and Change

Anything" by Kerry Patterson and many, many others. The Salvation Equation, in a sense, is a prequel or supplement to the body of self-help and motivational literature. This book will discuss universal principles common to all human beings that can be taken as an underlying foundation and then applied to any of the frameworks, techniques, theories and ideas found in other motivational literature. The Salvation Equation also establishes the foundations upon which thoughts and ideas of your divine nature that can be applied to whatever your daily pursuits might entail.

The Underlying Moral Imperative:

You are most likely in the majority in that you believe that you have one life to live, one chance to make the best impact upon yourself and the world around you. Like so many people, you also have an innate sense that you are connected not just to the world around you, but to a broader and more important purpose that transcends this world in which you live but is dependent on the actions and decisions you make here. Whatever our background and belief system, we can almost all universally accept the fact that we should maximize any and every positive opportunity we might create or encounter throughout our lives. Personally you probably feel an obligation to do your best, be your best and become your best. This is the root of a moral imperative that you must understand and internalize to gain the perspectives necessary to maximize your human and divine potentials. This is the core of the notion of a life well lived.

You should embrace the idea that if you are not striving to maximize your abilities and the outcomes of any given life situation, you are not living up to your given potential; you are falling short to some extent. You should seek to lift your vision to the core of you own divinity. You should seek and apply your highest possible potentials as you manage your daily processes and problems and seek to achieve. You risk limiting opportunities for your future growth or achievement if you are not doing the best can in the current moment or situation. You may unwillingly chain yourself to unwanted consequences of thought and action when you lose focus of your highest potentials.

While it is simply human nature to fall somewhat short of your absolute and highest potentials, the imperative demands that you at least strive consistently towards that goal. It is the direction in which you are moving that counts most. The steeper the ascent towards your highest potentials, the more fulfilling your life may become and the more positive impact you may have on the world around you. We all must journey forward; it is the essence of moral imperative to make that journey with appropriate zeal and commitment.

Perhaps what cannot be overemphasized is your internal motivation when it comes to internalizing the information in this book, understanding the implications of this moral imperative and activating your highest potentials. One of the side effects of living in this blossoming age of information is the fact that there is no limit to the number of voices that compete daily to try to tell you who you are or who you are not; what you are or are not; what you want or what you don't want; why you are or what you should be thinking. These messages are always vying for your attention, attempting to persuade you as to what should really matter to you and what should not. Behind all of these messages lies an agenda. Whether the agenda is positive or negative, useful or harmful is not for us to judge here. What we are concerned with is outlining and defining the common potentials we all share and applying those potentials to your own personal agenda that gives you the best possible outcome. As you begin to understand your highest potentials and the divine nature they imply, as you intuitively understand and operate from an ever deepening sense of self, you are empowered to create your own agendas. You are able to think, evaluate and act more freely within a fuller understanding of who you are and what your increasing capabilities consist of.

It is important to recognize that an avalanche of competing messages are out there, in the media, in our communities and institutions, among friends, family and peers, and embedded in the majority of daily activities. The sad truth is that the message that gets put across to you most effectively on either a conscious or sub-conscious level usually wins. It matters not whether the message was truthful, helpful, counterproductive, destructive or just designed to convince you to do something innocuous. Often lost in this cacophony of information is the quiet, powerful and influential nature of your inner voice, the influence that persuades you towards your highest potentials.

The most important aspects of your nature are not tied to your ability to be a better consumer or more informed on the latest entertainment, but rather are associated with your ability to become a kinder, smarter, more thoughtful, more accomplished and more loving human being. While you will always have roles to assume in your life, you will play those roles better, be more effective and more influential for the good of others and shape your world more positively if you utilize the highest degree of your own divine potentials. Further, the framework in this book attempts to give you a filter, based on your own ascent towards your highest potential, which allows you to interpret the numerous daily messages you receive and evaluate them in terms of those absolute potentials.

The primary impetus for internal motivation revolves around the fact that you are individually responsible for managing the process of maximizing your own personal potentials. The process cannot be subordinated to others. It is non-transferrable. It cannot be legislated or mandated by any religious tenet or government policy. You cannot be forced by any means or methodology to pursue your highest potential. You must simply and exclusively choose to do so. Nothing or no one else can make the choice for you. No law can be passed, no sermon can be preached, no social mandate can be implemented that could demand that you become all that you are capable of being. You have no one to rely on but yourself to activate your potential, and no one to blame but yourself if you do not. While the very nomenclature of divine potential suggests that you are never alone in striving for your maximum potential, it does not relieve you of the duty of choice. While outside influences may inspire or inhibit your perceptions of your ability to choose, the final decision is still yours. However and wherever you strive to activate your potential, it inevitably comes down to your own personal choice to do so.

Another dynamic you must also understand is that, in this world of increasing information, there are several types or degrees of information that you might relate or attach to yourself. It seems that much of the information we are exposed to is trivial and has little long-term use, such as the recent exploits of a celebrity or the score of a sports contest. While trivial information may be entertaining or briefly useful, it does little to activate or increase your potential. A more productive and useful category of information helps you sort and organize processes and phenomena, such as the Newtonian equation for gravity or a method for planting and growing healthier tomatoes. While this information is enlightening and helpful, you must filter it in ways that help you determine whether it contributes to your ultimate potential or not. The highest levels of information you may acquire pertain to those characteristics or principles that will affect and accompany you throughout your life and beyond. Examples of this higher level of information include the ability to obtain and share insights, opinions or empathy with another individual or the ability to feel love and act upon it in ways that lifts another or the ability to recognize the deepest levels of your own spirituality. This higher body of information and the principles that enable you to acquire it and apply it towards maximizing your potential are the primary scope and concern of the Salvation Equation.

The Salvation Equation is intended to arm you with ways of thinking, evaluating and understanding, both in terms of the empirical world in which you live and the intuitive or divine world that lay behind it, and help you to more effectively evaluate all of the information you receive. This allows you more ably to determine whether that information contributes to the achievement of your potential or not. If you are determined to internalize the assumptions and principles contained in The Salvation Equation, you will become more effective in evaluating the world around you, particularly in terms of information and ideas, as it relates to your own ability to grow and become your best. You will be more adept at setting and navigating a straighter course through existing oceans of information, ideas and perspectives, whether the waters are calm or turbulent. You will more effectively expand your own divine nature and its connection to the world around you. You will be able to more effectively categorize and process that which is of temporary use and that which is more lasting.

It might be helpful to picture your life as a play being acted out upon a large stage. As you are acting out your own personal drama we see stage hands, the Director, script callers and so on whispering to you from the wings of the stage. You are performing live and you are determined to give your best performance, but ultimately how the role is played is up to you. All of the voices whispering from the sides of the stage are there to provide you with cues and information, but whether they are helpful or not as to how you will portray your role is your decision. The Salvation Equation gives you a way of thinking that will allow you to execute your life's drama according to your best interpretation of your own personal script and help you sort through the many prompts and cues.

In this book, you will examine several principles and assumptions that are critical in understanding and unlocking the potential that is within you. You are a remarkable and complex creature. You are capable of incredible accomplishment and beauty, as well as incredible horror and destruction. You have the power of love or hate, enlightenment and ignorance, service and selfishness equally within your grasp. Your body itself is a marvel of biological engineering. Your heart and mind have capabilities that lie far beyond the ability to completely understand them in the time and scope of this life.

Philosophers, scientists, theologians and psychologists have pondered, analyzed and attempted to understand and categorize the human experience from our earliest beginnings. Here you will identify several core characteristics that you must assume have always existed within the confines of human experience in order to maximize your ultimate potential. The object of the

Salvation Equation is not to prove or disprove any particular doctrine or theory of science or theology. Rather, it is to equip you with a framework through which you might clearly evaluate and understand the many ideas that confront you and attempt to define who and what you really are. That framework will help you filter such ideas and information exclusively in terms of your ultimate potential.

Change by Degrees

The Salvation Equation implies personal adjustment or change. Taking potentials that may lie dormant or undiscovered and moving forward in a positive direction. Keep in mind that all change occurs in increments or degrees. Significant personal change is rarely an all-at-once experience. It begins with a change in thought, a development of perspective. These thoughts are translated into actions that become ingrained as habit. Good habits result in higher self-discipline achieved in day to day action which inevitably brings positive life results.

Rarely is such changed achieved through a momentary theophany. Life is made up of numerous "aha" moments where the lights go on and you discover something new and important. Patience and diligence is key in this process. These "aha" moments come more and more frequently as you act upon the inspiration of each moment and you build understanding linearly over time. They add up over months and years, but it is a gradual process. The greatest potentials within you may take years, even decades to refine and perfect. It is the small degrees of change, positive change, which repeated effort and understanding bring that make the biggest difference in the long term. Daily victories by tiny degrees should become one of your most precious mantras.

Think of your life, and the potentials that remain to be discovered and nurtured, as a marathon, not a sprint. In fact, think of it as a series of marathons with very little rest in between. As in any such race, the principle activity is to put one foot in front of another, step by step, mile by mile. And at some point you have completed the race. The absolute time it took is not that important in the race of life, it is simply finishing with the best effort you can muster. And then, depending on your circumstances, it is time to get ready for whatever course the next race may bring. Your mindset should be to face whatever race is coming with the same determination and focus, ready to run as required to reach the finish.

The Five Foundational Statements

The framework of the Salvation Equation revolves around five foundational statements that outline key assumptions involved. Each statement will help to progressively build ideas that enable you to come to a deeper and fuller perspective of your highest potentials. The concepts contained in each statement will be discussed in detail in subsequent chapters. These statements are the starting point of understanding that will help you reach toward your highest possibilities.

1) As a rational individual you must assume that you have a variety of potentials and you have the ability to choose to grow and expand those potentials over time.

2) To achieve your highest potentials you must assume that you are more than a biological phenomenon, more than just your physical self; there is a part of you that will endure indefinitely with organized intelligence and identity.

3) If you assume the existence of a higher, intelligent and divine Being who is directly connected to and interested in your potential, you will more clearly come to understand your own divine nature and the potentials associated with it in a larger, more universally enduring perspective.

4) If you are able to accept statements one through three, then you will feel motivated to prioritize your actions and values to activate and develop your most important and enduring potentials; seeking every available opportunity to exercise and expand those potentials to your benefit and the benefit of those around you.

5) Developing and nurturing enduring potentials will result in a depth of character and accomplishment that will contribute to living the fullest possible life and being prepared for whatever may come beyond this life.

With this introduction in mind, you can move forward and explore the principles of the Salvation Equation. Many of these principles may sound very familiar or be well known to you. Many of them may be new, revelatory or even controversial. The simple fact to keep in mind is that any person from any cultural, racial, religious, political or socio-economic background may choose to universally internalize and apply these principles. Though the specific avenues and results may vary, the ultimate outcome will be to activate and increase your positive and divine potentials. A group of people applying these principles becomes a more enlightened community. Communities applying these principles become a more enlightened state or nation. Nations applying these principles have the power to change and lift the world. But to change the world, you must start by positively changing yourself. The most useful priority in changing yourself is to explore the highest degree of your own potentials, and to maximize your own capacities and actions for yourself and for the betterment of those around you.

<u>Epilogue: The Two Possible Competing Models of the Universe</u>.

"I want to know how God created this world. I am not interested in this or that phenomenon, in the spectrum of this or that element. I want to know His thoughts; the rest are details. Science without religion is lame. Religion without science is blind". – Albert Einstein

Perhaps the epitome of scientific research, argument, theory and speculation is the origin and nature of our universe. With the advent of modern scientific instruments we have been able to peer farther into the known universe and learn more of the phenomena that occur within it. Yet with the expanding body of discovery and scientific progress, we continue to refuse to bring a coherent debate about the main two possibilities for the universe's origin. This subject clearly illustrates the chasm between secular learning and intuitive or faith based learning, and the need to bridge that chasm and give credence to both bodies of understanding.

After all is said and done, there are only two reasonable explanations that we can experiment upon. The first involves the scientific/secular origins championed by Carl Sagan, Stephen

Hawking and others. This model includes the Big Bang theory and many other concepts that remain speculative and unproven, but lend some credence to the current line of scientific thought. The other theory is that of creationists, also known as intelligent design in some intellectual circles. This model posits that an intelligence (God to the creationists) is behind the origin and order of the universe. It further states that laws and principles that guide the universe are based.

The first model, the secular "big bang theory" of random inception and evolution of the universe, is the most widely accepted scientific model currently. In this model any life, if there is other life and intelligence in the universe, would have evolved randomly along lines dictated by environment and random occurrences of physics and biology. Thus the bar scene from the original Star Wars movie or the foul creature from Alien becomes a possibility. Any type of creature or intelligence, aggressive, passive or benign, could theoretically exist in this universe. In an infinite series of random events, there could be an infinite number of possible outcomes. Stars, nebula, black holes, other galaxies and any other worlds that might exist are a simple mathematical probability as random astronomical phenomena dictate.

The second model, similar to the idea of "intelligent design", is that an intelligent being, who we will call God, is in charge. We work on the assumption that God organized everything and all creation answers to Him, for it is indeed His. In this universe, all creation and all life must answer to the same principles that guide our progression and potential. Any other dispersion or progression of life would suggest disorder and deviation from intelligent plan and principle; it would suggest a chaotic method of organization. And we would have to assume based on preeminent intelligence that God is a God of order. For any existence of consistent cosmological law implies order.

It is not unreasonable to expect God to put into place laws that govern the designs, creations and organizations that He has engendered. The discovery and operation of such laws and principles should indeed be the focus of the scientist. However, the origins of these laws is equally the responsibility of the true religionist. There is room for both outlooks in the quest for actual knowledge.

Under the model of intelligent design, the highest levels of intelligent beings would likely be very similar to us (perhaps with some minor variation) and would undoubtedly behave according to principles similar to the principles that guide the expansion of our own intelligence. In a universe of order and controlled design, any progress of other intelligences would be according to principles of eternal truth with respect to the faith and potentials required at our hands here.

There is an interesting declaration by (the then resurrected) Jesus Christ in the Bible that relates to this subject. In the Book of Matthew it states: "And Jesus came and spake unto them, saying, All power is given unto me in heaven and in earth", Matthew 28:18 (KJV) . That is an implicit declaration of universal power and authority, not just for this earth, but for all creation under heaven (meaning the known universe). If the there is no reason to doubt this declaration of Christ and we take his words and declarations at face value, for he is widely regarded as speaking nothing but truth, these words have profound implications for understanding the nature of our universe. He is saying essentially, "I am in charge and will be taking care of things both here and everywhere else". In a faith centric model, this is a direct confirmation that God is indeed in charge with a specific system of order within the known universe. Rational analysis suggests that one of these two models is correct. Which one are you willing to bet your future potential on?

Chapter 2

<u>Seven Basic Assumptions Needed to Identify our Divine Nature and Potential</u>

If you are like most individuals, you have often wondered about meaning and purpose to your life. You wonder how deep your heart can feel and how high your mind might reach. You wonder what your ultimate potential might be. You have pondered the nature of your origin and contemplated your ultimate destiny. Answers to these difficult questions require a lifetime of searching and experience. But there are steps that you can take as an individual to understand these questions more succinctly and point yourself in a direction that will eventually reveal useful answers.

Ask yourself the simple question: how can I establish a set of principles and assumptions that will lead me to the highest truths about myself? Philosophers have debated concepts of human truth and existence for centuries. Theologians use canonical writings and religious precepts to attempt to define the deepest truths. Political and scientific schools of thought seek to identify common underlying governance of human nature that can be held as universal. Yet after centuries of discussion, debate and devotion to various paradigms and modes of worship, there is still a wide range of disagreement as to what the true nature of a human being is.

In this chapter, a series of principles and assumptions will be put forth that may be internalized and integrated to serve as a guide, a directory as it were, to lead you toward the deepest truths of yourself and the highest perceptions of your innate nature. The Salvation Equation is not put forward as a body of doctrine that seeks to define such truth and divine nature, but merely is a guide, or set of signposts, to allow you to determine for yourself whether you are moving toward the discovery of the most important and truthful aspects of who you are.

The seven divine assumptions are designed to guide you toward the truth of your highest nature in terms of your highest potentials. It is necessary to first discuss four guidelines of what is meant by truth. This is not meant to make an ultimate declaration of what truth is or is not as the details of the truth of yourself is a very personal journey that you must undertake individually. An overview of certain guidelines of truth is necessary to understand the full power of the seven assumptions of your divine nature. In other words, you are asked to consider the idea that there is a universal set of guidelines that can help you define and understand what truth is, even though the identification and acquisition of individual truths is left up to your own unique experiences.

<u>Four Guidelines to Understanding Truth</u>

First, the idea of truth should, as a principle, exist independently within its own sphere of operation. This means that there are true ideas, principles or concepts that exist whether you experience it, believe it and accept it or not. For example, there has been much ongoing debate on whether other planets exist with an atmosphere and biosphere similar to earth. There is no concrete evidence that such planets exist, but the truth of the matter is that there are other worlds that now stand or there are not. The fact that no proof yet exists one way or another would not change the reality of the principle. Perhaps someday such a world might be discovered and possibly even visited, and that particular truth will be confirmed and become knowledge. Even so, if that day came, it would not change the actual principle of that particular truth as it now stands. If another planet with conditions like earth now exists, it will continue to exist whether we know about it specifically or not. The same concept applies to your divine and continuing nature. Your divine nature and continuing identity as an individual either has merit and exists as a true principle or it does not. In order to aspire to your highest potentials, it is imperative you assume that divine nature is an existing fact that will bear out its proof in its proper time.

Second, truth is something that has existed, does now exist and will always exist with the characteristics of its principles intact regardless of current perception or rhetorical persuasion. It is forever unchangeable. It is not attached to the latest trend in relevance or the persuasive argument of the day. It cannot be altered despite individual desires or impressions. This is particularly relevant to the assumption of the existence of a higher being, a concept of a living God. From our point of reference He has always existed, does now exist and will always exist or He does not. Your concept or perception of such a being would not affect the truth of the principle of His existence or unchanging nature, only His relevance to you and your actions.

Third, truth has a direct effect on each of us, whether you recognize it or not. Since truth exists independently, and becomes effective and relevant only when you are able to identify and internalize its principles, you are subject to it whether in recognition or ignorance of it. If you recognize truth and the principle behind it, you have the choice to accept or reject that truth to your own benefit or detriment. If you remain unaware of a specific truth regarding your intrinsic nature, you cannot have the opportunity to accept or reject it, therefore having no opportunity to reap the possible benefits of that principle and possibly suffering the neglects of your own unawareness. In any case, you are under the influence of the dynamics of truth, either to your enlightenment or ignorance of its principles. In the understanding of your most divine nature, you must recognize that if such a principle is real and active, if it is truly a part of you, it will have a dynamic effect upon you. Only your consistent and diligent pursuit of understanding that inner divinity can yield the benefits that lie in its very nature.

Fourth, truth can be universally internalized and shared on a personal level, although the implications and applications of truth are as unique and varied as we are. Truth may stand independently, be immovable and unchangeable, but it is felt, recognized and interpreted within each of us in a very unique and marvelous manner. What you do with the truths you come to understand is left to your own free will. You always have the personal choice to act upon truth as you understand it. When it comes to your potential and the divine nature of that potential, your internalization of truth, as you recognize it, shapes and colors the development of such potential. Pursuit of inner truth is a motivation, a yearning, a wanting, that if you are sensitive to it, you are compelled to pursue. It is that common wanting, the inner questions of the deepest truths regarding the intrinsic nature of self that has the ability to unite mankind in the most profound ways even if individual experiences and manifestations of such truths may vary.

The empirical scientist or the devoted humanist would point out that there is no empirical method to measure or quantify that which lies beyond the observable physical world. In this they are mostly correct. But the corollary that follows is problematic in that because the divine is not measurable, you must assume therefore that it does not exist (or is at least not significant to obtaining an understanding of yourself or defining the world around you). You must declare such things dogmatic, assigning these less tangible realities a vastly inferior status within intellectual thought. Such a line of reason discounts an underlying set of existing principles that can be universally applied and experienced by any individual.

The fact that the results of the intuitive or unseen vary from person to person does not render such experience irrelevant or purely dogmatic. The fact is that the mind and heart of a human being is not a test tube or machine where consistent repeatable results can be measured. You are infinitely complex and the outcomes you may achieve from any given input vary as widely as the individuals that process a common experience. That respective individuals rarely achieve exact, specific results from common inputs, either perceptually or behaviorally is not a reason to render such experiences meaningless or irrelevant. Human beings, in fact, do have common experiences and catalog them consistently in the process of building a personal understanding of the world through those experiences, both common and unique.

Much of the science and technology available today started out as an intuitive idea. A hunch; a spark of imagination that lead, through methods both random and scientific, to remarkable discovery. While the intuitive process does not dismiss the research, experimentation and hard work that must inevitably follow such inspiration, it is important to not discount the intuition that launched the whole process. If the visionary innovator can translate an inspired daydream into a set of assumptions that result in scientific application and invention, so you also can apply a set of assumptions about yourself and the divine nature within you into a set of operating principles that you can consistently apply to reach your highest potentials.

Almost any discovery starts with a set of assumptions. From these assumptions, you build a base of experimentation and data. You test the assumptions and data, all the while feeling them out. You try different approaches based on your assumptions to ascertain the truth or error of your intuition. This applies to the ability to discover your divine nature through your highest potentials. You must make assumptions and you must live by and test those assumptions consistently until you have secured a solid body of experiential data that eventually becomes experienced as knowledge. In the realm of your divine potential, the data you acquire is perceptual but measurable within the realities of your own mind. Over time, you will be able to tell whether or not the principles by which you live and the qualities you have developed by applying such assumptions have increased or been strengthened. With consistent application, you will feel emotionally strengthened, your understanding will increase and you will experience expansion of your intelligence, your senses and your confidence in your ability to function more effectively in any given circumstance.

If you are to achieve your highest potentials, there are seven basic divine assumptions you need to understand, internalize and apply to form a sound basis for understanding that which is divine within you. Without these assumptions, you will certainly be able to grow and contribute throughout your life. However, with these assumptions, you can activate the highest potentials within you and achieve levels of growth, motivation, understanding and perspective unavailable to those who would not apply them. These assumptions open the door to the divinity within you and point you to a path encompassing the highest and most profound personal characteristics. They awaken you to an intrinsic understanding of your divine nature and reinforce the fact that you are never alone in attempting to achieve your utmost potential.

<u>Divine Assumption #1 – A Higher Power or Being exists, traditionally known as "God".</u>

Most human beings are born with an innate belief in a power higher than themselves. There are many cases that have been identified, such as the interesting story of child art prodigy Akiane Kramarik, that confirm the idea that we come pre-programmed to aspire to and recognize that which is divine. While we would like to explain such things through social, religious or traditional indoctrination or conditioning, there are plenty of instances where such a sense of divinity contradicts the doctrinal environment in which individuals are placed. Whether an initial sense of the divine within you has been nurtured, ignored or programmed out of you through your cultural, educational and social references, you must begin with the basic assumption that a higher power or being exists. In this book, we will use the common Judeo-Christian nomenclature of God to describe such a Being. Whether you envision God as a distinct and embodied entity, a spirit or force that fills the immensity of space and time, or as an embodiment of power and principle, you must first begin with the assumption that He exists. While the perception of what His existence might mean to each of us varies as individually as we do, you must first begin at this point of common acknowledgement.

You cannot ascend to the lofty heights and aspirations of something you do not assume exists. If you are to even begin a set of thoughts or behaviors that can approach the divine, you must begin with an acknowledgement of the divine. You must assume that His existence transcends the type of existence you know here. You must assume that there is a part of His nature and understanding that far exceeds your own, but can at the same time understand and enrich you.

You must assume that He is an ideal towards which you may rightly aspire. The most elementary starting point is to entertain the profound idea that intelligence and understanding beyond your own does exist and will always exist, regardless of whether you recognize it or not. You must assume He can stand on His own and operate independently whether you regard His operations or not. You must assume that the existence of such a higher Being can only be of benefit to you and provide an exemplar for your own ultimate potential.

The arguments for and against the existence of God rage on uninterrupted. On the one hand, there are theologians and various peoples of faith as ardent proponents of Deity, often flavored by their concepts of doctrine and tradition. On the other hand, there are scientists and humanists who seek to abolish any acknowledgement or reference to something they cannot establish proof of, therefore mandating that no such power or entity must exist. Each side insists that they are right and that their argument is most valid. There is no intention here of attempting to prove or disprove the existence of God. Arguments either way are essentially futile, since any relationship an individual may have with that which is divine is a uniquely personal experience. It is non-transferable from one individual to another and must be arrived at individually and independently. While His existence is absolute in relation to each of us, the understanding of divinity varies in its nuances from person to person.

What is most important in the implementation of the assertions set forth in this book is that you adjust your mindset and your attitude to assume God's existence is real. Actions, behaviors, and the development of your potentials will follow in the footsteps of such an assumption. There are only two positions you can take. Either assume that the universe in which you live is a random collision of matter, laws and temporal development or assume that there is a higher intelligence that exists behind those laws and that there is, in fact, an order or intelligent design (and will) in operation. There is no middle ground. It is either one way or the other.

What these seven assumptions seek to establish is simply this: you will unlock parts of your inner self, your highest potentials, and then aspire to a deeper and more divine nature if you assume that God exists. You will not recognize or ascend as steeply towards the pinnacles of these potentials if you assume that the idea of a higher Being is fruitless or has no merit, as a sense of irrelevance of divine potential would accompany such a point of view.

<u>Divine Assumption #2 - We cannot assume to restrict God's operations or abilities based on our own experiences or perceptions.</u>

Organized religion and schools of philosophy have sought for eons to codify and define the operations and intent of the Divine. Through writings and histories, whether inspired or scholarly, religious leaders and other historical figures have attempted to bring the experience of the Divine within the reach and understanding of each of us. We tend to align ourselves, through family history, tradition or individual preference, with those ideas of God that are most familiar. One of the weaknesses of our attempts to break down the idea of God into simple and plain understanding is that we tend to place, through creeds, interpretations and traditions, limits upon what God is or is not, what He may do or not do, and how He may think or act upon our relationship to Him.

If you are to assume that God does exist, and that He indeed exists on some level above and beyond your own mortal experiences, then you must keep an open mind when it comes to placing restrictions on His operations and abilities. We all live in a three-dimensional existence, caught in the linear progress of time. Try as you might, your intellectual processes are limited by the linear nature of your current existence. You can only process one thought at a time. Indeed, your life consists of the linear progression of thoughts and learning, building one idea upon another, step by step. To assume that God's existence is also so restricted is to place boundaries defined by our experiences upon Him. This is not a helpful perception of the possible spheres the Divine operates within, and is an indictment on limiting our own possibilities of growth.

You must come to the conclusion that if God exists, and does indeed operate on a level higher than our own, that His operations and abilities lie beyond that which defines what you would describe as ordinary. If you assume that God exists at a level beyond our own, then you must also allow that He has a higher awareness and ability. If God could think of two things at once and act upon them, then why not four, or eight or an infinite number of thoughts and actions? To assume the omniscient nature of God is to also assume that he cannot be restricted by whatever definitions, creeds or dogmas may be assigned to His nature. Just as it is counterproductive to assume your own potentials have limits, it is not helpful to assume that God is limited or bound by the perceptions or descriptions men have attributed to Him. Neither assumption helps to open up the possible horizons of your divine potential.

<u>Divine Assumption #3 – God Loves you and cares about your ultimate potential; you have been placed in a position to act freely upon that divine potential.</u>

pg. 44

If you will exercise the assumption that God exists, the next step you must take is to assume that He is benevolent and interested in the increase and development of your divine nature and potential. This is a natural extension of the assumption that God exists and is a Being of highest intelligence. It also stems from the assumption that it is His intelligence or influence behind the world and universe in which we live. If there is an intelligence and order to the design of things, it follows that there should be an order to the management of such things. The primary principle of management of that which is divine is love. No other principle could regulate the highest levels of potential.

Virtually every major religion associates the idea of God with the idea of love. You should make the assumption then that it is unlimited intelligence guided by unconditional love that defines the dynamics of the universe, and anything of divine character within it. It is fair to say that if love were not the highest guiding principle of deity, then God would cease to be God. He would be something else, something far less. It is primarily an act of love that underlies creation and brings organization into being. It is love for all that can become that guides the principles of physical growth as well as spiritual growth.

You must always assume that an ultimate and unconditional love, a love beyond that which you are able to create from your own individual experiences, is behind everything that occurs around you. If God truly governs by love, then it is natural to assume that such love encompasses a concern for you to attain the highest possible potentials. Consider it as a law of mutual attractors. That which is divine in God supports and resonates with that which is divine within you. That which is within you as divine potential aspires to and reaches towards that which is consistent within God. The foundational principle behind all human potential and positive development must be unwavering, immovable and all-encompassing love.

One of the difficulties throughout history, an impediment to recognizing and developing the divine with each one of us, is the atrocities that have been perpetrated from time to time, either from one individual to another or one group or nation to another. When we do horrible things to each other, as the last century of global war has illustrated, many will lose personal faith in any loving idea of the Divine. They only perceive a morass of suffering and injustice.

But this is mistaken in that it conflates two opposing principles, that of unquestionable divine love and the equally precious and important idea of free will or personal agency. We are each free to choose our best or worst potentials. Service to one another is a positive use of potential, while murder, war and other bloodshed is demonstrably negative. If we are forced into any positive behavior we lose not only the crucial lessons of that behavior but any credit for virtue in choosing that behavior. We cannot learn love, especially the type that promoted our ultimate potentials, without the ability to choose love freely.

Such freedom to choose suggests that God would not intervene on a large scale (though in times of extreme duress many individual accounts of miraculous deliverance have been recorded that are attributed to divine intervention) if that meant the removal of our ability to choose. Even if that choice was of incredible devastation one to another on a tremendous scale. It is the divine nature of godly love that you should incorporate into your assumptions and worldview, not the flawed application of human frailty and error. Divine love implies that all such things will ultimately be balanced and justice will always be secured in the divine math of the universe. This is discussed more thoroughly in Assumption Number 7.

<u>Divine Assumption #4 – God's characteristics are predictable, consistent and knowable as you need them; He knows you and you can progressively learn of His Divine Nature.</u>

If you assume that God exists and that He is a being that operates from a foundation of power that is underwritten by love, you must assume that He knows you and He desires that you know and understand Him in a multitude of ways. You must operate with an understanding that the nature and characteristics of God can be known and comprehended insomuch as you need to and are able to internalize them for the purposes of activating your divine potentials. If God were to be completely unknowable, or to exercise conflicting inconsistencies in His nature or character, He would, again, cease to be God. If you assume that His intelligence is infinite, it follows he must know and comprehend everything about you, including your thoughts, actions and the ultimate potentials within you.

You live in a world and a universe that is governed by law and principle. It is the favored realm of the physicist and other scientific disciplines to search out, quantify and categorize these laws. Throughout scientific research and discussion, several laws or principles have been identified that guide matter, atomic structure, the behavior of light and so forth. In all of this research and the theorizing it inspires, there is a sense of order and consistency behind these laws as new applications are discovered. If the universe operates on consistent laws and principles, some of which have been discovered while many more remain yet undiscovered, you must also assume that the highest intelligence in that universe would also operate under consistent laws and principles. You must assume that God will see, think and act upon things consistent with the order and supremacy of His intelligence. From this perspective, He is unchangeable and unfailing. He will always retain the nature and character that a being of His omniscience should. If you perceive inconsistency or conflicting application of such principles in your concept of God, you should probably reconsider such perceptions of Him. Such a being would, by nature, exhibit no inconsistency or variance of character.

If God is thus immovable, you have opportunity to come to know those certain characteristics and consistencies from Him that introduce you to the divine within yourself. You need to be able to come to intuitively understand those divine characteristics that are relevant to you as they apply to the various purposes of your own life. You need to incrementally learn and understand that unchanging intelligence, love and concern for your ultimate potential is available to you if you but choose to seek it along your own spiritual journey. In other words, as His character and being is consistent with the highest laws of the universe, so you can develop your own potentials in a firm and consistent manner. If God fully operates within the realm of universal laws and principles, so you can develop within a framework of such laws and principles. If God displays His intelligence in a variety of profound and miraculous ways, you too can aspire to expand and apply your intelligence beneficially within the spheres of your own influence.

As beneficiary of the love and consistent character of God, human beings are organized with their own native intelligence and then placed in an independent sphere to act, choose and think for themselves. You can use this independence of being to choose to focus on whatever aspects of your existence you deem important. You are capable of contemplating, learning of and emulating a portion of the divine characteristics that God himself possesses and that can be reflected in the development of your own ultimate potential. You cannot be forced to take such a path. The independence and free will that you may inevitably exercise dictates that you will never be forced to consider the divine potentials within you. There would be no value and no virtue attained if you were required to choose and develop the highest qualities within you. The joy and the difficulty of developing your potentials are realized in the process you must go through to identify and choose those potentials completely on your own. While others around you may give support and provide a compatible environment for those potentials (or conversely create a difficult and contrary environment seeking to impede or limit your recognition of the divine), in every case you are still left to make the final choice.

Every person is also gifted with the tangible sense of conscience. We all seem to come with an internal compass that helps us feel and determine what is right and true to us and what is not. The degree of conscience can vary from person to person and from situation to situation. Some individuals develop an ever more acute sense of conscience as they learn and grow. Others, often through the operations of difficult circumstances and experiences, may diminish their sense of conscience. Your conscience is an internal guide, a quiet voice, which prompts you to feel and consider what might be right or wrong in a given situation. You can allow your conscience to be shaped and influenced by the events around you, but you can also allow your conscience to help shape you in light of those events. It is through impressions you receive via conscience that you can tune in to the quieter, more divine influences of a given situation. It is a reliable vehicle to discover the deep and subtle nuances of your divine potentials. If you nurture and listen to the whisperings of your conscience, you will discover one of your most dependable guides.

Soon you will be able, through application of appropriate assumptions about the nature and existence of God and through intuitive learning and behavior, to begin to understand the basic nature of the divine in God and in yourself. This process of recognizing your own divinity is not exclusively revelatory, although you will certainly have your share of "aha" moments. These are instances of clarity, understanding and insight that will be reinforced in your thoughts and feelings. You will receive, from time to time, moments of inspiration that whisper deeper meaning to your mind and soul. The meaning and significance of these moments will become very personal to you and shape your character. They will influence your thoughts and the development of your intellect. Although they cannot be measured by others, they will be very real to you. Despite these major touchstones along the path to activating your highest potentials, you will discover that which is divine bit by bit and measure by measure. As with most learning, you have to start with a fundamental foundation and build layer upon layer. You test each layer of learning and, upon discovering its benefit and application, add another layer of understanding based on experience. Learning of the divine within you is no different. It is a gradual and ongoing process.

It is inherent in this expansion of learning and a growing sense of self-realization that you can continue to build upon the divine potentials within you. Human beings are unique among all living things in the fact we are able to continually develop, modify, change and re-shape our concepts and ideas of who we are and what is important to us. This expansion of intelligence and self-awareness implies that the boundaries of your realizations can continue to expand. While you may have physical or mental limitations while living within this material world, should those limitations be eventually lifted, such as is suggested in many concepts of an afterlife, your progress would continue on in higher spheres of learning and growth. This continuance of intellectual growth, this expansion of your intelligence, coupled with unlimited time and resources suggests you can become something far greater than you may ever realize within the bounds of this life. What is the ultimate fulfillment of your potential when thought of in these terms? Would not such a process over time bring you into a clearer understanding of all that can be described as divine, both within you and from the very mind of God himself? Does it not implicate that divinity which is your inherited potential?

Divine Assumption #5 – You are able to possess a portion of divine characteristics.

Since you have been placed in a position to think and act for yourself and can experience an expansion of intelligence and self-awareness, you must then assume that you have been given a portion of divine character that is reflected in your ultimate potentials. If you assume that God exists and that He functions predictably and independently, administering and acting according to laws and principles that He established and holds immutable, you must also assume that your intelligence and the highest potentials you hold consist of and are subject to the same dynamics. If you assume God is a perfect being, you must assume that you can, even as a fallible and imperfect being, strive upwards toward a degree of your own perfection, or completeness. While you cannot be absolutely clear or certain what your absolute ceiling is in this life, you can aspire toward an upward direction and an increase in every part of you that reflects the divine. It is most important that you understand that it is the direction of your journey that is most important. Using your free will, you can choose to gravitate toward those characteristics that contribute to your own divine nature or you can ignore and drift away from them.

Your ability to think and act freely is what separates mankind from every other creation that exists. In a sense, your ability to think freely, to choose, to imagine, to weigh opposing viewpoints and to draw your own conclusions should be prima fascia evidence that mankind is more than just a material coincidence. It speaks loudly of a heritage that is above and apart from random evolution. It suggests very strongly that there is a superior intelligence behind our design and organization as living, functioning beings. It is not illogical to conclude that if our evolution and development were truly random that there would be more than one genus or species with such intellectual power and similar potentials. Yet there is only one creature, insofar as we know, that can even aspire to or quantify the essence of what they consider divine. That there are often so many differing viewpoints on the exact nature and function of the idea of "divine" only reinforces the point that we are unique in this quality.

You must operate under the assumption that you have at least the seeds of the divine within you. If God truly followed the biblical declaration of creating man in His own image, it must follow that you are naturally endowed with some portion of His divine character. In the pursuit of your highest potentials, you can come to recognize those attributes that make you noble and unique. You can grow and expand in ways that set you above and apart from any other organized intelligence. You can work and act in ways that acknowledge you have such capacities within you. You can elevate the vision of yourself and others to heights that the constraints of science and empirical logic would not otherwise allow you. What you can imagine, you can strive toward. What you can envision, you can labor to make real. If you can gain a vision and sense of divine characteristics within you, you will begin to intuitively understand how to reach for them and accentuate them in the very fabric of your being. You will begin to strive for the ultimate potentials that you may achieve.

Perhaps the most important facet of your divine character and your relationship to God is the assumption that a portion of who you are and what you actually consist of is above and apart from your physical existence. Call it your soul, your spirit or an everlasting continuation of mind. You will only begin to realize and understand the breadth of your highest potentials if you adopt a vision of yourself as something that will exist in an organized and recognizable form beyond this life. If you assume that a part of your identity, your thoughts, emotions and cumulative experiences survive beyond the span of your mortal life, you must change your perspective and shift your highest responsibilities toward yourself and others correspondingly.

Such a perspective forces you to rethink your priorities and what is most important to you. It demands that you focus more on those things that might actually transfer across mortal boundaries, specifically the development of a body of spiritual knowledge and an acute sense of the importance of positive relationships. The potentials associated with these priorities should receive proper attention and dedication. You will come naturally to an understanding that matters which are temporary and concern the basics of daily living are important and need attention, action and work. But matters that can remain with you far beyond your years in this world also need careful attention and nurturing as well. It is this perspective, the internalized understanding that comes from assuming your divine and eternal continuance, which opens doors to your highest potentials. To assume you are anything less than this is to impose artificial boundaries upon yourself in envisioning and striving for all that you may possibly become.

While science may not be able to provide absolute proof of the continuation of self beyond the physical life, it is most important that you operate under the assumption that an organized sense of self does continue on. This should become an absolute if you are ever to aspire to your highest potential. You must come to at least assume, if not completely accept, the fact that your mortal life is but a small chapter in a much larger journey. While science seeks for proof of such realities and the truths that lay behind them, you need to assume that proof will someday be established, and operate under the premise that the reality of your continuance is a given. While religion seeks to provide a body of doctrine or tenets that describe rules or conditions of your continuation, you should always work under the guise it is reality regardless of the nuances of its anticipated conditions or details.

<u>Divine Assumption #6 - You may always be empowered, from within and without, as you reach for your highest potentials.</u>

Once you understand and internalize the first five assumptions, you must come to the realization that you may always exercise the belief in your divine potential and empower yourself, as well as receive inspiration and empowerment from sources beyond yourself. You should always operate under the assumption that as you strive toward your highest potential, you will become empowered to eventually actualize those potentials. Your sources of empowerment can come from within, through self-motivation and self-realization, as well as from inspiration through outside sources.

You empower yourself by adopting perspectives that provide a larger and more complete vision of yourself and what you now can and eventually might be able to do. You begin to sense and understand the qualities of your divine nature and their importance. In turn, you begin to create rules and actions for yourself that reinforce your self-perceptions and move you higher in the pursuit of your ultimate potentials. The more complete a picture you develop of yourself and your positive and divine potentials, the more you will be able to contribute to your life and the lives of those around you. You will gain confidence in your abilities to grow, act and contribute. You will move forward with faith in yourself rather than fear. The higher your vision of yourself and the stronger your sense of the divine within you, the more you will feel empowered to think and to act.

You are empowered as you nurture and develop a growing sense of expansion of intelligence and self-awareness. When you come to recognize that knowledge is power, the more clearly you recognize the deeper realities of the world around you, and thus the more effective you become. As you continue to focus on the development of a specific potential you will eventually see the results of such labors. Your understanding of that potential matures and you become more adept at applying it. This empowers you to nurture and develop other potentials you come to recognize within you, moving you forward toward a more complete picture of self-realization and self-understanding. And so your potentials build within, step by step.

Your empowerment in your divine, positive potentials may come from without also. Empowerment may come from both those around you and from a sense of inspiration from power that lay beyond the physical realm. You hold within yourself the ability to either inspire and empower others or break others down, and they likewise can do the same for you. As a human being, one of the most precious assets you may have throughout your life is the love, comfort, support and friendship you can give to or receive from others. You have the ability through choice and focus to always look for the positive potentials in others. You also have the ability to contribute to others in various positive ways. The support, insights and timely feedback of a friend or colleague can often make the difference in a life-confirming or life-changing situation. We can simply be there for each other when it is most opportune. We can lift each other, love each other and serve each other. You can do this most effectively as long as your focus is turned to the ultimate realization of your positive potential and the importance of aiding others in reaching their potentials. With a selfless focus, you will feel compelled to lift and serve others, with attendant beneficial results.

The innate understanding that our potentials are interconnected and interdependent reinforces the ideal that selflessness is critical to the maximization of our own potential. When limited by self-centered focus, you may lose track of the needs and cares of others. When you focus exclusively on yourself, you risk losing sight of the needs and potentials of others. If you are obsessed with obtaining your own power, position, wealth or comfort at any cost, you lose sight of the fact that we are all interconnected in our quest for our highest and divine potentials. You cannot achieve you best absolutely alone. You cannot expand your sense of being within a vacuum. You must focus on equally empowering others to find the highest degree of empowerment within yourself.

Selflessness brings the capacity for growth and service, self-centeredness opens the door for neglect, abuse and the inevitable squandering of your potentials.

Further, you must also assume that if God exists and He is a being motivated by love while always desiring that you strive toward your highest potentials, then He will take opportunities to empower you toward those potentials if you will allow Him. In what forms, through which specific opportunities and how inspiration, insights and such empowerment comes may vary widely from person to person and situation to situation, but you must assume that empowerment through obedience to the principles that activate your own potentials will come.

Millennia of common experiences and millions of stories of inspiration and insight suggest that it has always been this way. To accept the nature of God as eternally unchangeable suggests that it always will be this way. The catalyst in your relationship with God and with your divine potential is contained in the simple effort to want to know Him and the divine potential placed within you. From the beginning of the simplest desire to want to know, without fear of what you may eventually discover, springs the beginning of empowerment toward your divine potentials. You simply have to choose to want to know the depths of your divine potential. You cannot fear what you might discover about yourself or the highest potentials within you. You cannot be afraid of inspiration and empowerment from sources beyond you. If you welcome the idea that you are never alone in the pursuit to be your best, you will discover constant sources of inspiration all around you.

<u>Divine Assumption #7 - You must assume you will be held accountable for the achievement of your ultimate potential.</u>

If you are to assume the existence, accessibility and the innate empowerment that lies within a higher Being or intelligence and you assume that there is a connection between this manifestation of God and yourself, you must inevitably conclude that there will be a point of reckoning and accountability to that higher power. You will be much more directly connected and aware of your progress and potential if you operate under the assumption that there will come a time and place where you must come under scrutiny and judgment for the recognition, activation and application of such potentials. Judgment associated with the laws of the world is the jurisdiction of governments and their courts and those who enforce such laws. These laws are not always enforced equitably and we, being human, make mistakes in their administration from time to time. Judgment of all of the nuances, possibilities and opportunities of your divine potential must inevitably lay in the wisdom and power of Intelligence and Being far superior to our own, One who is capable of exercising perfect justice.

If you assume that God exists and that He has all knowledge and power, then you must conclude that the application of that knowledge toward the evaluation of your potentials would be just, fair and equitably administered. You must assume that such a Being, operating under the eternal policies of unconditional love and benevolence, will fairly apply judgment, mercy and justice based on factors and contingencies above and beyond that which you yourself can imagine. Assume that He can see and evaluate your potentials from multiple and unlimited perspectives, bringing to bear the weight of what you actually achieve versus what you have the potential to achieve given your individual life circumstances. Further, you might assume that such a process of accountability and judgment would be the quintessential learning moment for you to come to a higher self-realization and prepare for whatever stages lay ahead in the progress and expansion of your intelligence and being.

How you might view the specifics of such a "judgment day" is not the most critical issue here. There are numerous cultural and religious ideas and traditions that elucidate such a time. What is important is that you recognize that if you assume such a process will eventually occur, and that it will be a fair and thoroughly evaluative undertaking, then you will develop a perspective that places the highest importance on how you progress in this life, how you use your time and talents and how you develop and apply your potentials for your own betterment and the benefit of those around you. The principle must apply universally. If you know you must inevitably give an account of yourself, you are more likely to be more diligent in how you conduct yourself preparatory to that accounting. And you must also assume everyone else will be held to the same standard that you will be.

This idea is a fundamental premise of the Salvation Equation. It challenges you to recognize that it is in your best interest to seek your highest potentials and do your best to identify and live up to them. If you work under the assumption that you eventually will have your day of reckoning, you can begin now to prepare for the examination. There truly would be no worse circumstance than to find yourself in a place and time where you become subject to such a process having been completely unaware that such an event was actually coming. It would truly be an eye-opening and uncomfortable experience. To work under a personal system of accountability, whether you choose to pursue it individually or through the tenets of an established institution, prepares you in many subtle ways to embrace the best potentials within you. It keeps you "on your toes" and provides introspective incentive to give your daily actions deeper meaning. If you try to see yourself in a broader light of accountability, you establish a brighter and clearer lens through which you may view the pursuit of those highest and most divine potentials.

Yet, this assumption should not be fear invoking, but one of empowerment. The idea of the Salvation Equation is to maximize the positive slope of your potential, and the corresponding divine assumption is that you will be accountable for that effort. But there is also the idea of mercy, assuming an all knowing and understanding God would be merciful. And the best envisionment of mercy is to assume that your accountability will be fair and that the purpose would be to reveal ways to increase your potentials, not judge them lacking and squash them forever. To be accountable is to be empowered to act freely and take responsibility for those actions. If the six previous assumptions hold true, you can only expect love, mercy and help in increasing and moving forward as that accountability is strengthened as you progress.

The seven assumptions in this chapter form a foundation for you to visualize and prioritize the most important potentials for whatever path you may decide to take in your life. The result of understanding and operating under these assumptions is that you will begin to think and operate with a broader, deeper and more far reaching perspective. You will begin to understand what you can be capable of beyond the ordinary daily maintenance of your physical needs and comforts. It enables you to expand your horizons and seek perspectives and priorities that will remain with you more than a day, week, month or year. It helps you begin to ponder and internalize those aspects and potentials within you that will become a permanently embedded part of who you are. It will stir within you the essence of all that is divine. You will live your life in such a way that you believe you can expand your potentials and progress, and that you know you will be empowered to do exactly that. The foundations of understanding that you build for yourself will be filled with more meaning. You can begin to come to an understanding of the idea that you are more than the sum of your biological makeup. You can begin to wrap your arms around the idea that there is a part of you which has been and always will be associated with the divine. You will begin to glimpse your deepest nature and highest possibilities.

These assumptions do not guarantee you the answers to life's greatest challenges or give immediate answers to your most intimate questions, but they can help you prepare. They allow you to see yourself and your relationship to the world around you in a more complete, meaningful and profound way. They help you develop a more sensitive perspective when life's experiences contain those teaching moments that prompt profound questions for which there is no immediate answer. They help you tune into the quiet, subtle and sometimes mysterious way that intuitive learning happens within you. They establish a powerful foundation from which you may begin to understand and explore all that is divine within you as you reach for your highest potentials.

<u>Epilogue: Two Orders of Mind</u>

Decades ago a famous Professor of Ancient Studies wrote a famous essay reflecting on the zealousness of the devoted religious individuals juxtaposed against the same individual's quest for true knowledge. His conclusions were simple, zealousness without proper knowledge (and wisdom) can lead to exaggerated and dangerous outcomes. Religion in the world today is spoken of both well and poorly due to some of the outcomes that a particular movement may engender without the proper considerations behind those outcomes.

In the essay the Professor describes two distinct orders of mind. The mind of man and the possibilities of the Mind of God:

"In one of his fascinating scientific survey books, this time dealing with the latest discoveries about the brain, Nigel Calder notes, "Two of the most self-evident characteristics of the conscious mind are that the mind attends to one thing at a time, and that at least once a day the conscious mind is switched off." Both of these operations are completely miraculous and completely mysterious. I would like to talk about the first of them. You can think of only one thing at a time!

If you put on a pair of glasses, one lens being green, the other being red, you will not see a grey fusion of the two when you look about you, but a flashing of red and green. One moment everything will be green, another moment everything will be red. Or you may think you are enjoying a combination of themes as you listen to a Bach fugue, with equal awareness of every voice at a time, but you are actually jumping between recognition first of one and then another. The ear, like the eye, is, in the words of N. S. Sutherland, "always flickering about. . . . the brain adds together a great variety of impressions at high speed, and from these we select features from what we see and make a rapid succession of 'models' of the world in our minds." Out of what begins as what William James calls the "great blooming, buzzing confusion" of the infant's world, we structure our own meaningful combination of impressions, and all our lives select out of the vast number of impressions certain ones which fit best into that structure. As Neisser says, "The model is what we see and nothing else." We hold thousands of instantaneous impressions in suspension just long enough to make our choices and drop those we don't want. As one expert puts it: "There seems to be a kind of filter inside the head which weakens unwanted signals without blocking them out. Out of the background of the mind constantly signals deliberate choices." Why the mind chooses to focus on one object to the exclusion of all others remains a mystery. But one thing is clear: the blocked-out signals are the unwanted ones, and the ones we favor are our "deliberate choices."

This puts us in the position of the fairy-tale hero who is introduced into a cave of incredible treasures and permitted to choose from the heap whatever gem he wants--but only one. What a delightful situation! I can think of anything I want to--absolutely anything! With this provision, that when I choose to focus my attention on one object, all other objects drop into the background. I am only permitted to think of one thing at a time, that is one rule of the game. An equally important rule is that I must keep thinking! Except for the daily shut-off period I cannot evade the test. "L'ame pense toujours," says Malebranche: We are always thinking of something, selecting what will fit into the world we are making for ourselves. Schopenhauer was right: "Die Welt ist meine Vorstellung." (The world is my idea or perception). But as to taking a calm and deliberate look at more than one thing at a time, which is a gift denied us at present. I cannot imagine what such a view of the world would be like, but it would be more real and correct than the one we have now. I bring up this obvious point because it is by virtue of this one-dimensional view of things that we magisterially pass judgment on God. The smart atheist and pious schoolman alike can tell us all about God--what he can do and what he cannot, what he must be like and what he cannot be like--on the basis of their one-dimensional experience of reality.

Today the astronomers are harping on the old favorite theme of the eighteenth-century encyclopedists who, upon discovering the universe to be considerably larger than they thought or had been taught, immediately announced that man was a very minor creature indeed, would have to renounce any special claim to divine favor, since there are much bigger things than us for God to be concerned about, and in the end give up his intimate and private God altogether. This jaunty iconoclasm rested on the assumption that God is subject to the same mental limitations that we are; that if he is thinking of Peter, he can hardly be thinking of Paul at the same time, let alone marking the fall of the sparrow. But once we can see the possibilities that lie in being able to see more than one thing at a time (and in theory the experts tell us there is no reason why we should not), the universe takes on new dimensions and God takes over again. Let us remember that quite peculiar to (modern Christianity) is the doctrine of a God who could preoccupy himself with countless numbers of things.

Plainly, we are dealing with two orders of minds. "For my thoughts are not your thoughts, neither are your ways my ways, saith the Lord. For as the heavens are higher than the earth, so are . . . my thoughts than your thoughts." (Isaiah 55:8-9.)"

The scientist will often deny the possible existence of God, the philosopher will seek to question the nature and actions of God while the religionist will attribute characteristics to God based on interpretation of scripture or historically formulated dogma. Yet no science or philosophy, at least to this point in the progress of human thought, can either prove or disprove the existence of divinity, either within each of us or an Embodiment elsewhere within the bounds of all existence. Ultimately, the issue must be boiled down to simple faith, and the assumptions that follow.

But clearly each of these approaches to the divine nature of God and man originate from our rather limited viewpoint. We remain, at least throughout our lifetime, trapped in the three dimensional restrictions of mortal, biological life, with the resulting limitations on our intellectual boundaries. Attempts at projecting beyond these realities are indeed the pursuit of the various parties according to their various methodologies, each attempting to attribute meaning to the entire process.

The significance of the Seven Divine Assumptions is to become empowered to reach toward a higher order of mind by forming a lens through which the existence of such an order of mind can be entertained and at least partially understood through our own inherent limitations. The assumptions in this chapter, once internalized, will allow a clear and consistent focus on the basic nature of Divine Mind. While it is clear we have no basis on which to make definitive absolutes on what God is and what He can or cannot, will or will not do, we have the basics from science, philosophy and revealed religion to at least work on a fundamental beginning point to adequately comprehend this concept of a much higher order of mind. And we certainly have the ability to embrace aspirations, based on our own potentials, to turn our minds and hearts at least in a direction facing towards a higher and more enlightened state. The Seven Divine

Assumptions are merely the first steps in ascending the staircase of possibility towards a more

divine state of mind through recognition of divinity within each of us.

Chapter 3

Overview of the Salvation Equation

The Equation Metaphor

This chapter explores the concept of the Salvation Equation itself. It helps to keep in mind that we live in a limited three-dimensional world, with finite concepts of time and progress that serve as checkpoints in our lives. We are always living in the moment. The past is behind us and we may not return there except in our memories. The future is ahead of us and yet to be written. What you have that is most real is the moment you are in right now. You have decisions to make and each decision affects, however minutely, the direction your life will take in the future ahead. In measuring the progress of your life you have to ask yourself regularly the question: "Am I doing all that I can do; am I becoming all that I can become?" It is fair to say we would all hope that the direction of our lives is trending upward, that by some measure we are becoming "better" or more complete.

With all of our various backgrounds and cultural, political and religious ideas that have been instilled within us, is there a way to envision the concept of "better" in a way that can be understood universally? We all have similar hopes, dreams and aspirations, despite the various avenues through which they might be manifest. We also all have the common ability to increase those potentials most relevant to us. We all have the capacity for growth, change and expansion of our most important potentials. Though our circumstances may differ, we can all envision ideas, events and outcomes that would lead to self-improvement and positively change our lives.

The Salvation Equation establishes a universal mathematical metaphor that provides a way to envision personal progress and a model that points towards your highest potential. As an intelligent living being you must assume that to truly live means to grow, increase and progress. If you examine your motives and life goals, you certainly would not feel the need to stagnate, contract or regress in any aspect of becoming who you ultimately want to be. Inevitably, you will progress in fits and starts. You will not always increase your potentials in a smooth or consistent manner. You will have alternating periods of progression, stagnation and regression, however temporary. The Salvation Equation is conceived to help you visualize overall progress toward all of the potentials you feel are relevant in aspiring to a life of fulfillment. It provides a simple model of evaluating, understanding and internalizing your highest potentials.

It also suggests that the very nature of your progress will point you ever more toward that which is truly divine within you, encompassing the deeper nature of your being. If you can envision a model for solid progress throughout your life, it should be natural to assume that the slope and direction of that progress must continue beyond the parameters of this life. The Salvation Equation suggests that the empowerment of your divine potentials lies in the simple fact that if you come to know you can progress in your potentials throughout your life, why should you assume that such progress ends with the termination of your mortal life? If you can move in a positive direction here, what evidence do we have that such progress would not continue if you assume that we maintain a coherent identity and state of existence beyond this life?

This perspective of continuance, an eternal perspective of self as it were, empowers you to think of yourself and evaluate your potentials in terms of what is most meaningful within such a model of continuance. It suggests that you should prioritize your potentials in terms of what has the most lasting value. It alters your perspective and takes you from a viewpoint of what is important only for the here and now, to a loftier vision of what is significant both now and in the distant future. It forces you to reconsider your priorities and to begin to think of what is most important to you within the broader idea of your perpetual growth and expansion.

The basic premise of the Salvation Equation is this: If you understand and take advantage of every possible opportunity, both self-created and randomly discovered, and utilize each of these opportunities throughout your life to maximize your personal growth and potential, you should be able to achieve the maximum accomplishment and outcome associated with taking full advantage of those given opportunities. Your actual performance should at least approximate the opportunities you have encountered. These concepts can be illustrated by creating a graphic of the equation for a line.

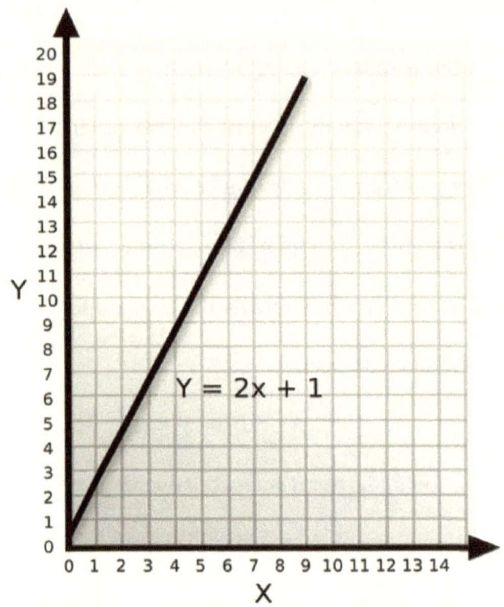

Illustration Graph of a Simple Line

The standard equation for a line is y=mx + b. Think of the progress and development of the potentials in your life as a linear process within the time you are allotted (again, we live in a linear world). The Salvation Equation illustrates your ultimate potential versus your actual progress throughout your life. The equation is stated thus:

$$\Delta Y = \sum (M[b] \rightarrow M[d])\, X[o] + B[p]$$

Visualize your progress and actuation of potentials throughout your life in this simple mathematical metaphor. The Salvation equation helps to visualize and plot the progress of your potential where:

ΔY= Degree of *change, progress or fulfillment* of our total potentials, both human and divine. This encompasses the degree of your self-realization and actualization in applying your potentials.

$\sum M[b] \to M[d]$ = The sum of the acquisition, recognition, development and application of your *total potentials* from the time of birth until the time of death.

$X[o]$ = Value of the given points of *opportunities*, both self-generated and randomly happened upon, throughout your life.

$B[p]$ = The *starting point of latent potentials* you possess when you are born. In other words, talents that may come "pre-programmed" within you.

$\Delta Y(v)$ = An illustration of the average of progress made throughout life to the point of death. In a perfect world, while living a perfect life, you seize every opportunity that you encounter and apply yourself perfectly to each opportunity, enhancing your own potential and enriching the lives of everyone around you that stands to benefit from your actions. Such a flawlessly executed scenario describes your absolute life potential, which is labeled $\Delta Y[a]$, or the highest possible degree of perfection and fulfillment you could achieve having lived a perfect life:

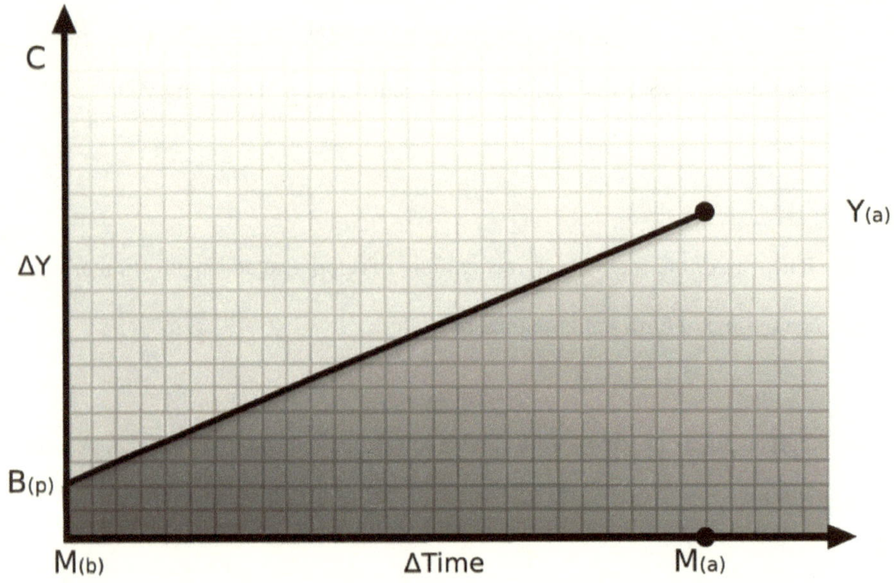

Illustration of straight line graph showing ΔY absolute (ΔY[a])

One significant problem is that we all live in an imperfect world. Often your best intentions meet with mediocre or irrelevant results. Sometimes you achieve remarkable successes. Other times you must cope with dismal failures. You can never completely control the outcomes you desire. What you can control is your own cognitive ability to move forward and upward in your desire to realize your highest potentials. During times of setback, disappointment or difficulty imposed upon you, always make the choice to move forward and upward regardless of your circumstances. When you find yourself trending downward in some aspect of your life, always seek to change your direction and move forward and upward again.

You have the power and ability within you to choose your direction, even if you cannot always control the outcomes of your actions or the actions of those who may affect you. An illustration of a life well lived should approximate the slope of your absolute change in potential, your $\Delta Y[a]$. While it will be virtually impossible for you to achieve every possible goal, aspiration and potential that you possess in one lifetime, internalize the concept of moving your potentials along a similar slope, a similar life path to the potentials and opportunities you are given. It would be unreasonable to think you could perfectly and fully achieve your $\Delta Y[a]$, but your final and ultimate assessment should reflect every effort to approximate and reach towards that $\Delta Y[a]$. In other words, if you were to measure the actual progress you have made throughout your life, would the slope of that progress look favorable in terms of the absolute potentials you might achieve?

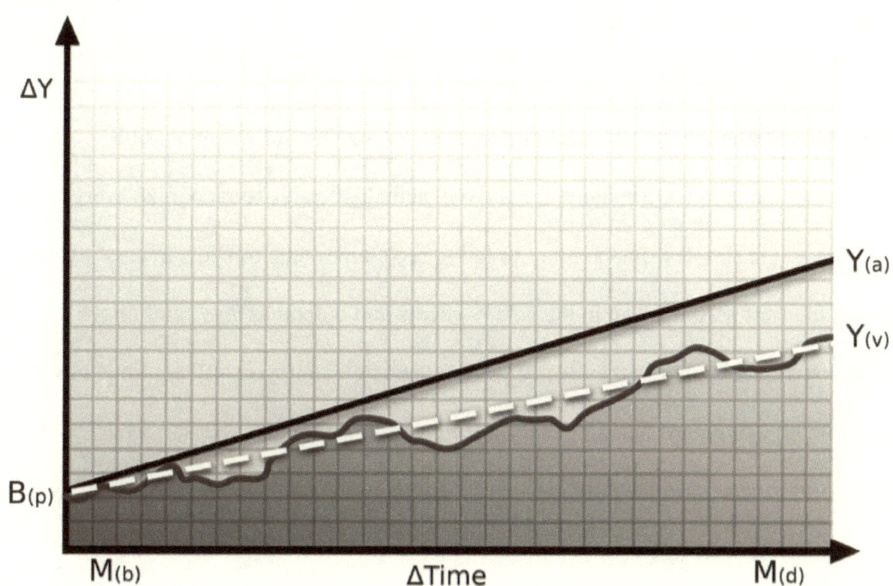

Such a graphing and illustration of the progress of potentials would describe an exceptionally well-lived life. Again, your goal should be to have the actual progress of your life $\Delta Y(v)$, in terms of achieving your potential, approximate the ideal slope of $\Delta Y[a]$ as closely as possible. This suggests constant progress and refinement in the process of self-evaluation and self-realization. It demands that you continue to move forward and upward in developing and actuating every possible potential you may discover. It intimates that you strive each day to seek the best you have within you, applying yourself relentlessly to the development of your potential and the achievement it might engender. Yet, it can be observed that while there should be a consistent upward trend in development, there are periods of stagnation or even decline. Despite the set-backs suggested by times of flat or negative slope, the trend is ever upward, ever reaching for the best within you, ever trending towards all that you might become.

This is the metaphoric realization worth striving for, the maximization of every possible opportunity you might be given. Ultimately, no one will actually be able to recognize every possible opportunity. It is simple human nature to fail to recognize some of life's interesting and pivotal moments, thus not participating in the achievements and outcomes they might have provided. But if you are dedicated to the idea of your highest potential, you will continue to work on developing yourself and grasp each and every relevant opportunity that you do recognize. The closer you approximate your ultimate potentials as described by $\Delta Y[a]$, the more you may lay claim to the ideal of a life well-lived.

In achieving your highest potentials, always remember that such achievement is not accomplished in a vacuum. Such a path of life achievement illustrated above involves the interaction, synergy and support of many other individuals that cross your path, interacting with and inspiring you along the way to your highest potentials. It also involves identifying and operating under the assumptions that guide your divine nature, reaching for inspiration and assistance beyond yourself. It involves receiving and integrating inspiration from within and without, plotting your upward progress in terms of the many "aha" moments you will log throughout your life.

Many of the opportunities you will encounter involve the chance to lift and be lifted by those around you. We are constantly in orbit around each other, influencing each other in obvious and subtle ways. You can see whatever you choose to see in others since you constantly carry the dynamic of developing potentials in either a positive or negative direction. You have opportunity, wherever you are, to learn, grow and feed off of others if you will allow yourself to do so. If you are focused and dedicated on developing your own highest potentials, you will constantly be concerned about the highest potentials in others since you know your quest for achievement will create interaction and effect upon others. If you choose to see the highest and divine potentials within others as well as yourself, your attitude, regard, respect and ultimately your treatment of them will correspond with such perspective and attitude. If you choose to synergize your highest potentials with others whenever the opportunity presents itself, you ultimately accelerate your own progress as well as enhance the progress of those around you. It is important to keep in mind that you are never alone in your quest to expand yourself. You will find many other like-minded individuals if you choose to look. You will find inspiration and motivation from unexpected places and in unexpected ways if you will simply choose to focus and move forward and upward.

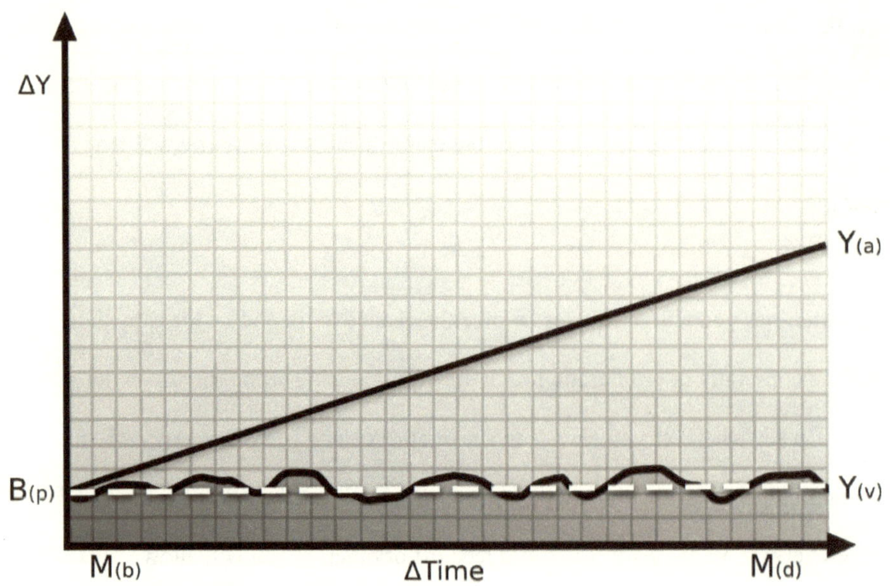

Illustration of graph showing ΔY absolute with neutral actual life slope ΔY(v)

The above graph illustrates a life path in which higher potential was not sought nor maximized. The difference between the ΔY[a] and the actual achievements is described by a wide disparity of slope. Such a description of attitude and actions towards maximizing each life opportunity could be best described as "unmotivated", "laissez-faire" or "mailing it in." A continual lack of improvement or development of potential would be considered basically just biding one's time as the world passes by. A passive approach to your potential is detrimental in a dynamic world.

pg. 76

The more you decide not to progress, the more you are falling behind what you may become. You are losing in a footrace against yourself toward a distant finishing line. There is no neutral ground in life as it relates to the progress of potential. You are either developing potential or you are losing it over time in relation to where you should be. There is very little that fits a description of "in between." This will be discussed at length in Chapter 6. The more opportunities you miss, the less progress you ultimately will make. If you are not looking for opportunity at all, any progress of self-realization and development of potential is obviously limited.

Perhaps one of the greatest hindrances to achieving your ultimate potential is achieving only a small portion of your potential. We often seem, as individuals, to be resistant to change. We enjoy finding our "comfort zones" in life. We get comfortable with achieving a little and saying to ourselves "it is enough." The worst enemy of developing your progress is to grow a little and become satisfied that you have done all that you can, when you have actually just begun to scratch the surface. Again, the world we live in is very dynamic. It is changing all of the time. We are dynamic beings, always changing and becoming. You must continually adjust and monitor your attitude and progress to assess whether you are reaching upward, sliding downward or just idling along. Achieving your highest potentials is a daily process. It is a constant renewal of dedication, self-evaluation and self-realization that you are what you have become, and you can become much more than you now are. You must remember that each day you awake you can determine that you will improve incrementally in whatever areas of your potential you deem relevant.

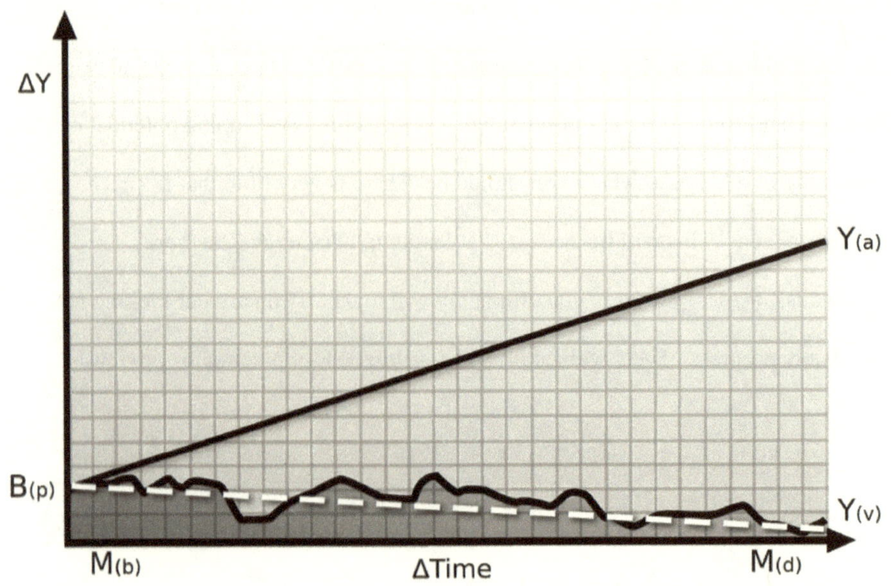

Illustration of graph showing ΔY absolute with negative actual life slope

The scenario that should be avoided is neglecting your potentials or utilizing your potentials in an overwhelmingly negative manner. If you develop yourself in such a way that you exploit your potentials for a personal benefit or result that creates a detriment for yourself and/or those around you, you define your potential with a negative slope. You are not expanding but shrinking if the underlying foundation of your potential growth is not rooted in absolute and unconditional love. Love of self, love of principle, love of knowledge, love of all that is divine and love of the potentials of others must be in balance. In order for your potentials to have positive growth, your actions in developing that potential must have innate benefit to others should they become part of your personal sphere of influence. Any pursuit of personal power, influence, wealth, knowledge or information is only positive when the acquisition of such potentials is focused not just on the benefit to self but on the betterment of all. This is not to say that the blessings of developing your potential for your own benefit are innately negative. It is the motivation, intent and the stewardship over the effects of your own potential that inevitably counts. It is both the manner in which you pursue your potential and what you do with the fruits of your work towards your highest potentials that matter most.

In conjunction with the divine potential within you, the dynamics of unconditional love and concern must permeate all that you do to maintain positive direction of your potentials. The broader nature and definition of such love will be discussed in Chapter Nine. When you undertake a path to expand yourself that directly results in your own or someone else's suffering because of your actions, you reinforce a negative slope for your potential. This is the equivalent of fostering a zero-sum mentality, which occurs when one person believes that what they must obtain for themselves can only be gotten if they put themselves ahead of or at the cost of another. True potential, especially divine potential, is unlimited in its scope and availability. It is free to all and has the capacity to be synergistic to all. The more positive and divine potentials you achieve, the more opportunity you create for others to achieve their potential also. We are all inescapably intertwined in our pursuit of our highest and most divine potentials and are therefore accountable not just to ourselves but to each other. We cannot escape this dynamic, the principle remains active and has effect on us all, whether we choose to recognize it or not.

<u>The Direction and Slope of Your Potentials</u>

The truism "attitude equals altitude" could not be any more applicable in any of these cases. You are free to form attitudes toward your potentials in any manner you choose. You may choose not to adopt the attitude and desire for achievement, expansion and growth; you may choose to see no point or value in it. You can choose to watch your life pass you by, striving for only the occasional passing desire or want, hoping you do not have to exert yourself too strenuously to obtain it. Or you can choose to look around you and seek to identify and achieve every potential that could enlighten and lift you and others around you.

You can choose to turn your quest for your own potential into a self-centered clamoring for only that which might benefit you no matter the cost to others. Or, you can choose to seek to grow and expand everything you feel to be good about yourself and look for opportunity to share such knowledge or achievement beneficially with anyone who might be interested. The cumulative effect of your attitudes and the choices that result from them over time will inevitably influence the slope and direction of your potential. There is little neutral ground when it comes to the slope and direction of potential. You are either engaged in growth, self-realization and self-expansion for your benefit and the benefit of others, or you are occupied in an exclusionary, self-centered pursuit for your own benefits without consideration of the cost to others.

This does not discount the difficulty of living in a world where you are often incented to look out for yourself first. You are surrounded by political, social and economic systems that suggest the more you achieve and accumulate for yourself, the better example or superior talent you are attributed. The direction of your slope is determined primarily by the attitude of inclusiveness you develop as your own potentials are discovered and pursued. Are you using your potential to make the world as you know and understand it a better place? Does the development of your potential enable you to bring out the divine within yourself and others? Does it provide a clear path to expansion of your abilities, influence and knowledge that you intend to use for the benefit of any and all within your sphere of influence? Even if the sphere of influence is just yourself for the moment, will there be opportunity in the future to include, lift and enlighten others with what you have developed and discovered? Is your motivation or process underlying the development of potential viewed as a strictly personal accomplishment for your own good at the exclusion of the possible benefits to others?

These considerations will all influence the slope and positive or negative direction your potentials will take. Again, our potentials are intertwined. You cannot complete yourself and achieve your highest potentials without allowing your potentials to benefit any and all who fall within your sphere of influence. Neither can you be truly be complete without experiencing the positive influences and potentials of those around you. The highest value of our potentials must encompass our influences upon each other.

<u>Positive and Negative Potentials: A Four Point Test of Principle and Application:</u>

Central to the Salvation Equation is a four point test that can be applied to ascertain the positive or negative slope of the development of your potentials. The development of your potentials in a positive direction has been emphasized, with an underlying assumption that your divine potentials are the highest and most positive of all. You can apply a simple four point test to determine if the recognition and development of a potential reflects a positive or negative slope. To reach your highest possible potential keep in mind that the steepness and direction of the slope relative to your $\Delta Y[a]$ is critical. You should always be progressing with a positive slope indicative of increased personal attitude, desire and development towards fulfillment.

Test #1 – Does your potential bring greater self-realization and personal growth?

As the first and perhaps most important test, you must be able to determine if the development of a desired potential helps you to grow and progress. You must be able to sense continual progress over time. Can you look in the mirror daily and honestly say that your actions are making you smarter, better informed, more intelligent, more physically fit or whatever quality your potential engenders? Your progress as an individual, including all aspects of your ultimate potentials, is incremental in nature. It comes a little at a time in most cases. You may occasionally have those "aha" moments when a strong dose of insight or self-realization hits you, but the usual course is a little progress here and a little there. The development of potential is a study in time, persistence and consistency.

Like a budding and growing plant, you need to feed, water and nurture the potentials within you. They need the sunshine of opportunity and a fertile field of interrelationships to blossom and grow. You will realize the fruits of these efforts over time if you consistently feel more self-aware. You know you are growing your potentials positively when you can self-evaluate and come to the clear understanding that you are currently more because of the process of nurturing a potential than you were a month, a year or a decade ago. Some potentials are easily measurable, such as the time it takes to run a mile, or the progressive ability to work and solve complex math equations. Other potentials are not as obvious or easy to measure. Your capacity to love takes a lifetime to nurture and perfect, if it ever can truly be mastered in such a brief period. Or the ability to increase your sympathy toward others may find formation and outlet only when inspired by a specific traumatic event or series of events. You do not always have control of the timeline of events that will provide just the right opportunities to develop your potentials. What is important to focus on is the results of becoming more self-aware and more of whatever potential with which you are concerned.

You can assess your progress toward the positive through the monitoring of your ability to think clearly and respond naturally and efficiently in a situation that requires application of your potential via specific skills. For example, if you have been training to run a mile long road race, you can evaluate your progress while running week by week with a stopwatch. When race day comes your body's response to the strain of the race can be felt physically and intuitively. Your time across the finish line gives a specific measure of your success or failure based on your goals and expectations.

While other potentials may be much more subtle, you can still look inwardly and sense growth and progress. If you are sensitive, you can feel a growing sense of ability and empowerment as you develop an important aspect of your potential. You can measure, for example, an increase in your knowledge of important skills at work. For example, your job might require that you develop both leadership and empathy in order to supervise other employees through a difficult set of tasks. You can feel your responsibilities over time, which your practice and application of these skills sharpens, becomes easier and more natural to execute. You then grow in confidence through experience as you apply your potential through specific exercised skills in daily situations. You first believe you can do it, you do your best and apply your potential consistently and diligently, and with the passage of time and experience you come to know that you can do it. When you see positive results and gain confidence within yourself, when you reflect and realize measurable growth has come, you understand clearly that you are moving in a positive direction.

Test #2 – Is your potential applied fairly and beneficially to you and those within your sphere of influence?

As discussed earlier, the biggest litmus test to determining the positive vector of your potential is whether or not your application of it is fair and beneficial to everyone involved, including yourself. In your development of that which is most noble and divine within yourself, you must always keep in mind that you do not live in a vacuum. You are constantly influenced, shaped and acted upon by others. You constantly influence and act upon them. At times, you may never fully know of the influence or effect you have on the lives of others. Often, your influences may be manifest immediately, but the cumulative effect of higher levels of actions on others might not be realized for days, months or years to come. It is, again, the critical measure of self-centeredness versus selflessness. You must develop your potentials with the idea that you must first expand and grow, nurturing your innate potentials in preparation for beneficial actions and applications. Second is to share those potentials for the expansion of growth of others in any way possible, bringing progress and benefit to all involved.

The intrinsic development of positive or divine human potential suggests by its very nature that you would reach out to include as many as possible within the parameters of that potential. Whether you have a natural psychological need to be recognized for that which is best within you, or whether you operate from an idealized position of service to others, you should always be reaching and striving to use your potential for mutual benefit. If you have a capacity to gain empirical knowledge and utilize it skillfully, and you know it has broad and useful application, why would you not share and encourage others to develop such similar paths of knowledge? Might you feel the desire to teach and train others in that area or potential that enriches all? If you feel the benefits of fitness training and the strength of body and clarity of mind constant training yields, would you not encourage those you know to find their own best levels of fitness? In almost any circumstance imaginable, your own potential is enhanced when you have the opportunity to serve, encourage and benefit those around you.

You should always undertake the process of putting yourself in the mindset of others within your sphere of influence whenever possible. You can practice trying to see yourself and the potentials you develop through the eyes of others, of trying to anticipate how they might see and react to you. You may be your own harshest critic, but you should always entertain the insights, feelings, feedback and influence of others when conducting self-evaluation of the broadening impact of your potentials. If your actions are perceived as fair and beneficial to those around you, you can assume in confidence you are developing your potentials in a positive manner. You can also assume you will deepen and enrich those relationships that are affected by your positive efforts.

Test #3 – Can the potential be consistently and repeatedly applied with positive outcomes?

Consistent and constant upward development of your potentials should yield consistent and positive results as you act upon those potentials. Repetition and constant practice with an eye on improvement will, in most cases, bring positive and reoccurring results. If you are able to obtain repeatable positive results in developing and applying your potentials, it is safe to conclude that you are progressing in a positive direction. Because development of your potentials is usually more of an intuitive than empirical process, you cannot always expect exact and consistent results. There are simply too many dynamics outside of your control, including the people and circumstances in which you find yourself. Nevertheless, you should observe similarity and consistency over time in all that you do, even taking into account outside or unseen influences that may impact the exercise of your potentials.

In the example of running a timed mile, you can plot your progress week to week and month to month simply based on improvement in your times. Measurement of your deeper and more profound potentials is less exact, but equally important and meaningful. The key is a constant desire and attitude towards improving your potentials. When you see positive results from your actions, you are motivated to continue forward and seek additional similar results. If you subscribe to the mantra we are all creatures of habit, the best habits we can develop are those that would constantly nurture the highest potentials while encouraging positive and uplifting outcomes.

Test #4 – Is your potential a characteristic you would want to see continue throughout your life…and beyond?

The final test for any potential you might discover and develop is simply this – is it important to permanently integrate that potential into your very being? Is it something that you can envision becoming a part of you, enriching you and changing you for the rest of your life? Is it an aspect of your character that you would hope would survive beyond this life and remain integrated into your being in whatever state you might find yourself in a life after mortality? Further, do the lifelong actions of your potentials leave a legacy for those around you that will encourage the pursuit of their own potentials? Is your corner of the world a better place due to the exercise and expansion of all that you could become? In other words, does the development of a particular potential create value that you can see as enduring, or at least be beneficial for as long as it might be needed or enjoyed by you or anyone you may have influenced? For example, an improved mile time is a potential that has a definite shelf life in its scope and application. Increasing your logic or your empirical knowledge has a much larger and longer scope of application. Developing the capacity to expand your intelligence or to love unconditionally has a possibly unlimited scope and application and the power to change lives.

If you are truly seeking to activate the highest and most divine aspects of your potential, it must be assumed that such potential would remain with you as long as you exist. Imprinted upon your soul and integrated into the very thoughts and fiber of your being, both temporally and spiritually. It would leave a history of positive results and influence on any and all that knew you. It would set a foundation for generations to come that may build upon the potentials you have exercised. It would, in its own way small or great, contribute to the growing library of knowledge and experience leaving an indelible mark on humanity.

A simple phrase summarizes the value of highest potentials for your life and beyond: You take with you only that which you have learned and the wealth of those whom you have loved. It behooves you to seek, envision and develop all those potentials that would contribute to such outcomes. The exercise of the highest and divine potentials within you enriches and describes all that you may become and the legacy you will leave.

<u>Chance versus Created Opportunity</u>

Your potentials are activated and realized within the framework of opportunity. Opportunity may come to you in many forms and in many unanticipated ways. For example, opportunity is created through adversity as well as prosperity. In general you can group your opportunities into two main categories – random or circumstantial opportunities and created opportunities.

Random opportunities are the most common. Life's twists and turns are almost always unpredictable and most often unforeseen. Frequently, you may not see an opportunity that falls right in front of you. Sometimes you feel that fate or chance always seems to smile on someone else – "some people have all the luck." In the development of your potential, the utilization of opportunity as it is presented directly affects the steepness of your progress. The more opportunities you recognize and pursue, the more you have a chance to discover and activate your innate potentials. While you may feel that others have more luck, more breaks hence more opportunity, you are only accountable for the opportunities that you may or may not recognize when they are encountered. You need only be cognizant of those opportunities to which you find access and eventually can exercise a degree of control over. You will encounter opportunities that can give you a chance to grow and develop, you simply may not have control over when and where the best opportunities might occur.

The second type of opportunity is the created opportunity. This occurs most often when you apply yourself in a current opportunity and create other corollary opportunities from it. Thomas Jefferson once stated, "I find that the harder I work the more luck I seem to have." Work and effort are often the precursor to greater opportunity. The more you seek to apply yourself, the more you attune your desire toward accomplishment and maximization of your potential, the more likely you become to discover additional opportunity through which to develop potential.

Whether you open your own doors or stumble through a randomly opened door, be sensitive to the opportunities that are presented to you. You may not become a multi-millionaire, but you can learn the value and satisfaction of work or the rewards of a wise investment. You may not become an Olympic miler, but you can learn and enjoy the benefits of exercise. You may not become a famous statesman, but you may find opportunity to enlighten the local town council. You may not publish poetry like Longfellow, but you can write and record the important impressions or events that occur in your own life. Your ability to recognize opportunity in its many forms is critical to finding an outlet for your latent potentials. The more you take advantage of opportunities you recognize, the more opportunity may seem to find you.

In considering the many ways in which you may encounter opportunity and reviewing the Salvation Equation conceptual graphs above, you need to ask yourself several critical questions:

* Am I taking advantage of every opportunity I recognize and am I maximizing those opportunities based upon my abilities and circumstances?

* Am I recognizing with each opportunity a chance to develop and maximize my personal potentials based upon the specifics of the given situation?

* Can I perceive a benefit of learning and/or action within each opportunity I am presented with?

* Can I see opportunity in the difficulties and failures encountered as well as in the triumphs and achievements?

* Do I come away enhanced by each opportunity and have I found specific ways to benefit myself and others through it?

Your best efforts at seizing the day, at finding every possible opportunity that you may encounter, are the catalyst for progress in your potentials. Always have your eyes open and your heart and mind ready to make the best of whatever opportunities are presented to you. You cannot always predict the when, where and how of a given opportunity. What you can do is be prepared to embrace opportunity when it does come.

<u>The Cost of Inaction</u>

Whenever you do not recognize opportunity as it comes or whenever you choose not to embrace opportunity or develop the potential it engenders, you face a difficult consequence. Because you live in a dynamic world, a world where change is constant and where there is little neutral ground, if you are not moving forward and developing your potentials, you are actually falling behind. Every opportunity missed creates the possibility of widening the gap between your actual achieved potential and your $\Delta Y[a]$. Stagnation or lack of any measurable progress is the same as losing ground on what you have the given chance to become.

You must be ever cognizant of the fact that your life is constantly in motion and your intellect and soul is constantly open, fluid and dynamic. You are responsible for managing the daily choices you face. Day to day, hour to hour and moment to moment you are constantly confronted with the decision to act or not to act. The responsibility falls directly upon the individual, YOU, and no one else. Both choices carry consequences. The choice to act upon an opportunity can carry positive or negative consequences depending on your intentions and attitude toward the potentials in action. The choice to not act carries almost universally negative consequences when action and application of potential would yield a more positive result.

Many of your actions may seem routine to you, but in truth, there is little routine to the choices you must make each day outside of daily personal maintenance. The growth of your potentials is reflected in the fact that it is not necessarily the importance of your choices that change over time. Rather, it is the growth in your ability to recognize, process, classify and execute the numerous choices you must make on a daily basis. Your application of choice and the positive development of your potentials within each given choice make you stronger and wiser. Inaction makes you weaker and ensures you are losing ground on the progress you could be making. This is a liability you should not be willing to entertain, if you truly understand the possible long-term losses in potential that result from a pattern of inaction over time.

<u>You Can Always Change Your Slope</u>

If you reflect carefully, you must conclude that you are responsible for each decision that you make, whether they are for your benefit or detriment. There is always the opportunity, moment to moment, to change your decisions and the direction of your potentials. You have the power and the ability to recognize an area of your life where your potentials are lagging or falling, and turn those potentials into a positive and into progress. While you can outline reasons or conjure up barriers to the process of positive change, inevitably it stills comes down to that specific individual decision.

Every minute of your life offers the ability and opportunity to point your path for potential upward, ever closer to your $\Delta Y[a]$. This is a part of yourself, and one of the few aspects of your life, that you truly can have complete control over. It is one of the few things you can do with confidence and utmost competence if you so choose. Every minute of every day you have the power within you to change the direction of your potentials, and ultimately the direction of your life. You cannot hold anyone else responsible; you are the final source of your own personal change. When it comes to accountability in the performance of your actual potential to the possibilities suggested by $\Delta Y[a]$, you will stand alone when it comes to the specific decisions of establishing your direction.

In the final analysis, it is indeed the direction that you are facing that is most important. How can you competently and adequately classify a "good" or "virtuous" or "upright" person compared to a "bad" or "hurtful" or "wicked" person? The Salvation Equation suggests that the difference lies in the direction and slope of your cumulative potentials. If you are developing positive slope to your potentials, you are creating benefit for yourself and others. If your potentials are sloping decidedly negative, you will undoubtedly be engendering more harm than good. The sum of your character can be defined simply by the direction you are heading.

The eventual outcome of consistently working toward every positive potential that you choose to recognize and activate is a greater wholeness of self. The application of all positive human potential transforms you into something more. It molds you into something greater, something transcendent, something approaching divine. But that greatness begins each day with the individual decision to reach higher and keep moving forward in positive growth and development. It begins with a desire to choose those actions that will create positive slope in each and every thing you think or do. It begins with a simple desire to face and move upward.

Epilogue: The Universality of Mathematical Models

Galileo once stated: "Mathematics is the language in which God has written the universe." Math is indeed a universal language that can, once the symbols used in math are learned, communicate across any cultural or faith based paradigm. Plato iterated: "The highest form of pure and universal thought is in mathematics." The idea of a math problem, even when used metaphorically as it is in The Salvation Equation, can be understood by the largest number of individuals.

Obviously the swath of human emotion and experience is far broader than simple equations, but the idea and concept of human progress is most effectively encapsulated in such a mathematically based symbol. Progress is progress, whether it be numerical or personal. Einstein captured this thought when he said: "Pure mathematics is, in its way, the poetry of logical ideas." Bertrand Russel also expounded on the idea of existence being experienced mathematically when he said: "Mathematics is, I believe, the chief source of the belief in eternal and exact truth, as well as a sensible intelligible world. Physics is mathematical not because we know so much about the physical world, but because we know so little; it is only its mathematical properties that we can discover."

And at some points in our existence, mathematics may even encompass and transcend our daily experiences. Euclid stated: "The laws of Nature are but the mathematical thoughts of God."

No matter where you might find yourself at any point in life, if you step back and think of personal progress from a mathematical point of view, specifically the linear equation of slope and progress of potential, you can establish bearing points. You can create a viewable and accessible illustration of where you think you are and what direction you want to go.

Positive and upward progress is the natural slope of a human being. Every system and power of which we are comprised strains to grow, progress and expand. The metaphor of the linear equation captures this phenomena in a simple and illustrative way. A way that reaches across any culture, religion or political affiliation.

Chapter 4

A Three Part Model of a Human Being and the Key Potentials Within

Historically there have been numerous models and ways of viewing and seeking to understand the complexities that comprise a human being. Any model that can cause reflection and deep personal introspection is useful. Any doctrine or principle that can clarify human nature and lead to a deeper appreciation of true self while motivating to higher growth and achievement is helpful and positive. This chapter examines a three-part model of a human being, exploring the mind, body and spirit as separate but interrelated parts, discussing the key potentials that primarily apply to each.

While these three aspects are discussed individually, these three areas overlap and affect each other in the development of almost every potential. They are interrelated parts of a greater whole, looked at individually to enhance your understanding of each. The model helps you identify and envision innate potentials, both temporary and enduring. Potentials of the mind and body will serve you well throughout your life if they are positively developed. Potentials of the mind and spirit have the ability to not only expand and grow throughout your life, but to survive and endure beyond. These potentials form the core of your divine nature.

The potentials outlined in this model are defined as those traits, powers, abilities, characteristics and possibilities that you may personally access and develop if you so choose. A specific potential contains the entire sphere of possibility of that characteristic or ability and the actions it may engender that you are ultimately capable of achieving. Every determined individual has access, whether through an inborn innate ability or through acquisition due to environmental or situational life experiences, to recognize and activate any and all of the key potentials outlined in this model. The potentials that you choose to recognize and develop will shape your life, your character and give flavor and direction to your every experience. The broader the spectrum of potentials you pursue, the fuller, more fulfilled and more complete your life may become if you choose to utilize those potentials in a positive manner.

The Salvation Equation covers the key potentials that you may develop. It implies that developing potentials moves you forward in a fulfilling, useful and productive manner. It suggests that positive activation of potentials builds your character and allows you to more effectively contribute to your own well-being and the good of others. The key potentials outlined all imply application in a positive vector or direction. This implies beneficial growth and expansion of self-results from activating and developing these potentials. Each positive potential creates emotional and intellectual synergism, empowering your thought processes in a way that promotes recognition and activation of other positive potentials.

The more of your innate potentials you seek, the more you will continually find. Potentials complement and build upon one another. Each positive potential you internalize will enlarge your capacity to recognize and understand other positive potentials. Accumulation over time of a broad spectrum of your potentials reveals a more comprehensive understanding of your more enduring and divine nature. It enables you to view yourself in a much broader sense than just biological realities. But just as you have the capacity for positive growth, there are negative possibilities to potentials that can result in the internalizing of negative and harmful attributes.

You live in a world of applied opposites, and you can easily make choices that would direct your ultimate potential away from your highest $\Delta Y[a]$. For every positive application of a potential, there exists a corresponding negative application of that potential with a negative value and vector that can inhibit your development. Where love can exist so can hate. Where intelligence can be developed so can ignorance. Where a sense of reverence might exist so might disrespect or abuse. Where logic can be sharpened, so might confusion, deception or a lack of mental discipline. Where you can develop habits that lead to good health, you can also develop behaviors that lead to disease or even death.

Through your ability to think and act freely, you can choose the direction and vector of the potentials that will define your life. You can choose to understand and act upon your potentials in a manner that will lead you upward in the quest to be your best. Or, you can just as easily choose negative applications of your potentials that will limit or destroy your abilities to progress, think and act as an independent being. Indeed, positive potentials are liberating while negative potentials are confining.

As you internalize each area of the model individually, keep in mind that these three aspects interlock, overlap and are inescapably intertwined in all that you experience and do. The spirit, or soul of a person, is housed in a masterful biological creation known as the human body. The mind, or intellect, is best viewed as a merger of both sprit and body with much of its activities housed within the parameters of the human brain. The body is best viewed as an entity driven by the mind and tempered by the spirit while functioning as a receptacle, or home, for each. Although specific potentials are categorized for each part of the model, your highest possibilities for achievement and a fullness of life lies in activating as many potentials within each area as possible.

Keep in mind that the development of every potential of which you are capable builds and strengthens you in the situations and roles you chose to assume in life. Whether you assume the role of father, mother, spouse, brother, sister, manager, employee, friend, lover, mentor, leader, disciple or judge your dedication to developing all of your positive potentials will enhance your ability to execute those roles and have a greater effect upon yourself and others. Over time, the exercise of your potentials in a positive direction creates expansion of all of your faculties and abilities; it refines you and polishes you in marvelous and unexpected ways. It creates a broader, more expanded understanding of what you may become. It allows you to perceive, comprehend and approach your deeper, more intuitive and more divine nature. It is a viable path to an understanding of your highest possibilities and an increasing completeness of self.

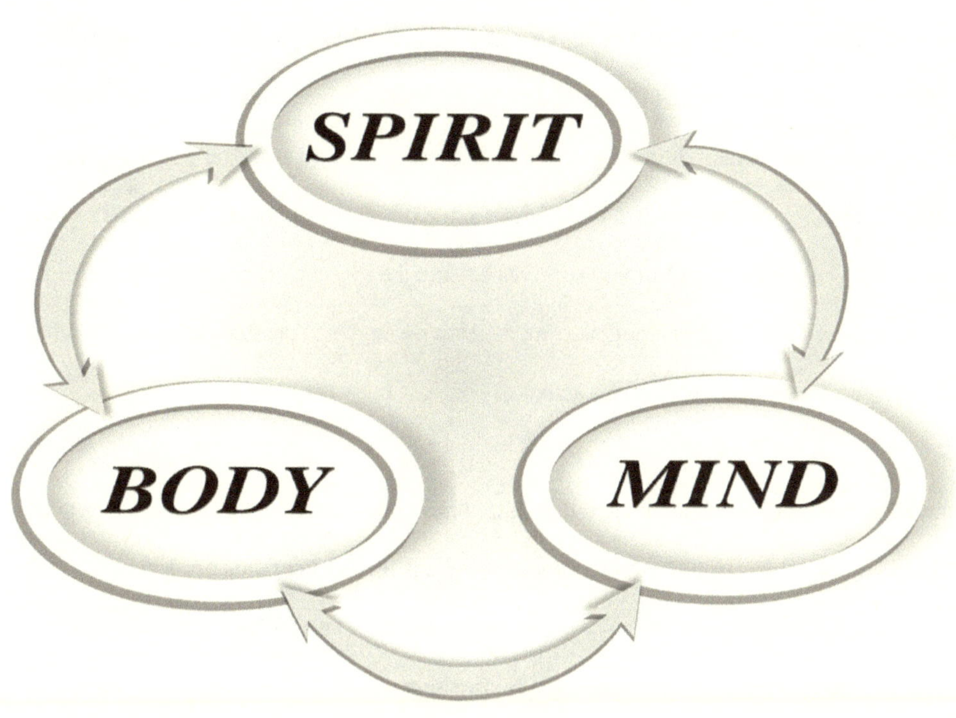

Illustration: Spirit, Mind, Body

The Spirit: In order to truly set out on a path that maximizes your potential, it is critical to assume and eventually come to internalize that a human being is more than just a sum of biological parts and processes. Although it is the jurisdiction of science to examine the precise nature and functioning of the human body, it falls within the spiritual or intuitive discipline to comprehend that we are something more than just a complex composition of natural elements.

It is not the intent here to argue the proofs or justifications for the existence of a tangible spirit or soul. Rather, it is to imply that to maximize your potentials it is imperative you assume and eventually accept the proposition that there is a part of you that functions and exists beyond the realm of your basic biology. A part of you that will survive and surpass the eventual decay and death of the body, independent of itself, yet tied to and affected by your physical senses. This, above all else, points to the importance of the assumption of our divine nature. For you must conclude that if you assume a part of you survives beyond the eventual demise of your physical body, it becomes critical that you recognize and develop the highest potentials associated with that part of your transcendent, divine character.

The human spirit or soul is acknowledged throughout most cultures and religions. The nature of the soul has been the focus of philosophers and theologians for as long as history has been recorded. In the Far East, the mastery of the Chi, or inner soul or energy has been taught and refined for several millennia. In the west, we subscribe to mainly Judeo-Christian concepts of the soul. While neither science nor theology has developed empirical proof to identify the exact nature and substance of the soul (although a scientific argument could be made based on the laws of conservation of energy and matter), it is nevertheless important that you assume it plays a central role in your personal development. You must assume that your sense of self is incomplete without it. There are specific, intangible and intuitive feelings and thoughts that you experience that can best be explained by attributing them to spiritual substance versus mind or body only.

While the journey and state of the soul beyond life is not within the scope of discussion, the nature of that spirit, the intuitive makeup and character, is relevant. There are key potentials associated with the spirit you may feel have come "pre-programmed". These are seemingly inborn gifts that you may unlock at various stages of life and come to fully integrate into your larger picture of self. By recognizing the existence of an inner spirit, you are identifying a part of you that serves as a repository for specific intuitive feelings and perspectives.

There are many times in your life when you may have an "aha" moment. These moments come as sudden flashes of insight, sudden realizations of facts or truth. In these moments you may find your understanding and insight suddenly enhanced and increased. While you might argue that you retain these flashes in the biological repository of the mind, the origin of these moments can be seen as a culmination of ideas, feelings or realization of self which had no previous direct mental or physical association. You may categorize these intrinsic moments of discovery as spiritual insight. Whether the origin of such information comes from within or from a source outside of you is not the critical issue. It is important that you experience these moments from time to time as they are often significant in scope and meaning. These "aha" moments become pivotal touch points in the discovery of self and the potentials you may unlock. They distinctly and gently alter the course and direction of the slope of your development, pointing you towards your $\Delta Y[a]$.

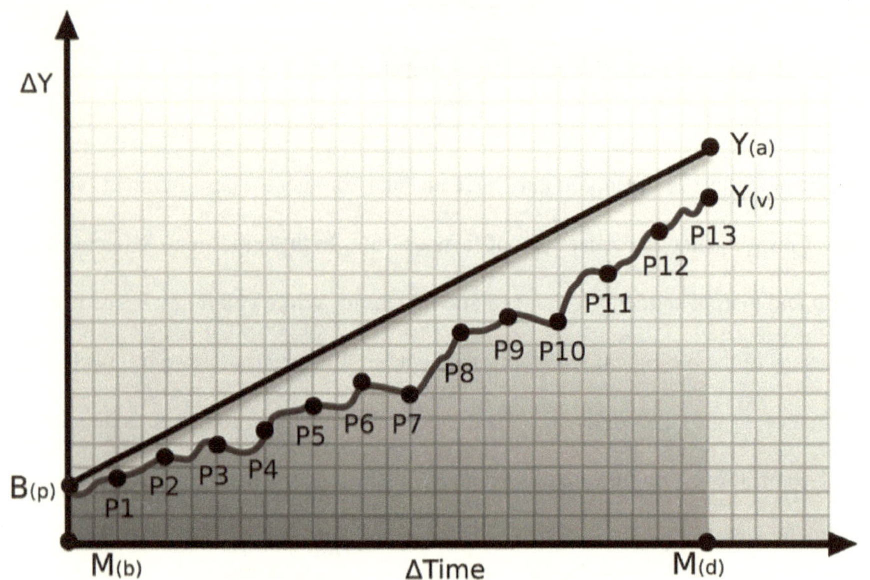

Graph of Potential with identified pivotal moments

The spirit is the foremost piece of this model. Within the spirit lies the most numerous and the most important potentials, those potentials which point to your continuing and divine nature; those potentials which are most critical to develop and endure. While the mind and body function as conduits through which these potentials are exercised and refined throughout a lifetime, the most meaningful growth ultimately lies within the realm of the spirit. If you assume that this is the only part of you that has continuation, then you must also assume that the potentials the spirit has achieved, and the information that has been imprinted and retained upon it, are the most critical. These would by definition be the only potentials that survive and transcend this life.

Further, if you assume a continuation of being and existence beyond this life, you must logically conclude that all that transfers across such a boundary would be the enduring knowledge, cumulative emotional experience and the development of personality and character that you have accomplished through your actions and relationships while alive. Therefore, the divinity of your character is directly determined by what you have learned, how well you have loved, and the cumulative effect these potentials have ingrained upon you and others. You should seek to devote significant time to the acquisition and development of these potentials, operating under the constant assumption that they will refine and prepare you in the most significant and profound ways.

<u>Key Potentials Associated Primarily with the Spirit</u>:

The Capacity to Love: The first potential that is traditionally associated with the heart, soul or spirit of a person is the capacity for love. Love is an incredibly broad subject that encompasses and defines the highest levels of interpersonal and environmental relationships. Love is broken down into many sub-categories or types of love: romantic love, parental love, love of nature, love of physical objects, childlike love, etc. Your capacity, focus and development of the ability to love on many levels will affect your life and shape your destiny more than any other single potential.

Love should be viewed as the highest, most transformative and most motivating emotion. It is experienced as the strongest force that bonds you to those near and dear to you and to the world around you. In its most wholesome forms, love creates families, friendships and relationships that may survive for generations. Love is the cornerstone for strong individuals, families, communities and nations. Despite all of the emotional capital that has been invested in love throughout the ages, love can be defined in a very basic and accessible manner. Love can be viewed in its purest form as a decision, whether conscious or subconscious, to put the needs and abilities of another to become and reach towards their ultimate potential equal to or ahead of your own. This is the core principle of your capacity to choose to love.

When you make such a decision and commit to nurturing the potential of another, you are attaching the highest positive value to your actions and potentials. When you act out of a foundation of love, selfless concern reinforces your decisions to act and you regard others in a compassionate and concerned manner. It is critical for your expansion and progress that you work out of a mutual foundation of love; love of self and the potentials that you might contribute, and love for those around you whom you have opportunity to uplift, and a love for all that may be considered divine within us. Constant application of love in the development of all your potentials unlocks insight greater than the experience itself. As your capacity to love grows, your innate understanding of your true greatness, the divine possibilities within you that may come to be realized, become clearer.

Understanding and developing your capacity for love is the first and foremost priority of all of your positive potentials. This will be discussed more broadly in Chapter Nine. You allow all of your positive potentials to grow and expand towards your highest $\Delta Y[a]$ when you operate on the basis of unconditional and all-encompassing love. A person with a love and passion for learning will apply themselves more readily to the acquisition of knowledge. A person with a love of a particular sport will practice harder, play with more zeal and pleasure and ultimately come to a greater understanding of all the dynamics involved in that sport. A person with a true love of music will listen, appreciate and play a particular instrument with more meaning. You will achieve more, retain more and appreciate more of your positive potentials when you are consistently operating from a foundation of love. It is the power that drives all positive actions. It is the potential that enforces the qualities and character of all that is divine within us.

Capacity for Intuitive Knowledge: You can divide acquisition of knowledge into two main categories, intuitive and empirical. Empirical knowledge is the domain of hard science, where repeated experimentation can yield measurable and consistently quantifiable results. Intuitive knowledge is an understanding or association you develop over time through experience, mental and spiritual. Intuitive knowledge is the internal recognition and meaning you distill to help define the less tangible facets of the world around you. Intuitive knowledge is owned by you individually as it carries the unique imprints of your own personal experiences and perceptions.

You will often rely more on intuitive understanding to define, categorize and understand the world than you will on empirical proofs. Intuition often suggests that there are levels of understanding that lie beneath what you perceive as obvious, or that may transcend or supersede the hard and specific experiments of science. You cannot always quantify this knowledge, yet you internalize and understand it. For example, it may not always be simple to give specific examples of "beauty", you simply know beauty when you see and experience it.

Intuitive knowledge is a potential developed mainly through the spirit. You accumulate impressions, feelings, and unique experiences and form conclusions over time about their meaning. While empirical proofs are generally set within boundaries, intuitive knowledge can expand, change, develop and mature in scope over time depending on the variety of experience. Intuitive knowledge forms a filter through which you identify and give value to perspective and insight, such as what might constitute "moral", 'happy", "dangerous", "uplifting", "exciting", "outrageous", "sacred", "excessive", "boring", "virtuous", "ludicrous", "inspiring" or "insightful". It is through this filter that you assign value to ideas and experiences. It allows you to more acutely determine what is meaningful and worthwhile and what is not.

Even though it is difficult, to measure this potential is critical in the development of your inner spiritual self. It is important to understand that intuitive knowledge is almost never absolute. It changes, grows and broadens over time according to the cumulative nature of your experiences and the maturation of understanding that follows. Some of the assumptions and impressions you have cataloged from earlier experiences may be superseded by greater understanding from subsequent experiences. For this reason, the empirical world discounts these "changeable experiences". But in self-development, they should not be considered unimportant. Your capacity to develop intuitive knowledge serves as an important reference point for other spiritual potentials as you strive to learn and grow.

Capacity for Discernment: Similar to the capacity to develop intuitive knowledge, but worthy of a categorization of its own, is the capacity for discernment. Discernment is the ability you possess to distinguish between fact and fiction, truth and error, right and wrong. Discernment is the intuitive ability to perceive and internalize these distinctions. Intuitive knowledge can be gained from the lessons of experience. This ability is one of the most crucial in the development of spiritual potential, but one of the most difficult to refine.

We have a tendency to view truth and falsehood through the lens of culture, traditions and education. However, most people have an innate sense of right and wrong, a sense that rises above simple moral platitudes or the cultural training we have undergone. Through the careful development of your own spiritual impressions and application of conscience you are able to build a model that creates useful categorizations for truth and falsehood. It is common to believe that there are absolute truths that cannot change or be changed; truth that stands independent and unchangeable, wanting to be acted upon. Other types of truth may be seen as relative and changeable depending upon time, circumstance or new understanding on an issue. However you perceive that which becomes true to you, your highest potential is dependent upon your ability to recognize and act upon truths that have meaning, and meaning that can be sustained over time.

A simple illustration of discernment can be found in the golden rule. "Do unto others as ye would have them do unto you". This simple statement is a call to a moral truth of behavior towards other individuals. You may initially view it as a guideline and internalize and act upon it with generally positive results. By acting upon the principle repeatedly over time you can first discern, then apply and then evaluate the strength of the principle as a guiding truth. If you continually apply the principle with continued positive results, the truth of it is confirmed within you. Your discernment of the correctness of the principle shapes further decisions to act. Actions that bring positive results confirm the positive vector of the potential and the correctness of your initial feelings. Over time, you actually become that principle, never seeking to act upon another in a way you would not want to be acted upon.

Capacity for and Control of Emotion: It is fair to say that life can be described as primarily an emotional experience. You begin from your infancy to experience a wide array of emotions, starting with hunger and fatigue and building through the years to an indescribably broad spectrum of feelings. It is also fair to say that at some point you will have experiences that expose or elicit nearly every possible human emotion. The gamut of emotion, just like your potentials, can be categorized across continuums with opposing values that are associated with positives and negatives. You can experience joy and sorrow; pleasure and pain, elation and disappointment, trust and suspicion, excitement and boredom, security and peril, love and hatred, faith and fear, certainty and doubt, confidence and anxiety, bravery and cowardice, peace and uncertainty, tranquility and turmoil. With every emotion you encounter, you have the opportunity to develop the ability to internalize, give value to and inevitably focus and control that emotion.

This potential has been developed to a high degree when you can effectively control and focus your emotions rather than be controlled by them. You are always acted upon by your emotions, but you also always have the choice as to how you translate those feelings into behaviors. It is the dimension of mastery and control of your emotions under any given circumstance that defines the positive development of this potential. Understanding the range and strength of your own emotions and the emotions of others within a framework of control empowers you to empathize and uplift when necessary. With discipline of your emotions you are able to operate from a position of strength in utilizing abilities and potentials within given situations that require specific decisions and action. With emotional mastery, you are in a position of power and control and can act accordingly. You are able to discipline your actions and focus on those actions that bring positive expansion of your potentials and the potentials of others.

Capacity for Reverence: Reverence is defined as the ability to see and understand a deeper or more divine and transcendent meaning to the events and circumstances around you. Having a reverent attitude or perspective suggests that you look beyond the obvious and see higher or deeper purpose. It also suggests a dimension of respect and awe for such greater meanings behind life's experiences.

There are fairly universal impressions that have inspired people to reverence throughout the ages. Reverence for deity, nature, the universe, heroes, political or social leaders, family, friends, certain ideologies, memorials or life itself are themes that are common to most any country or culture. Reverence is a sense, a feeling and perspective, that there are higher or more divine insinuations to life's events that resonate deep within you. It can be a spiritual experience to just sit out underneath the stars on a clear night and observe the constellations or the Milky Way. You can sense a profound power in the smell and beauty of a perfectly bloomed rose. You can discover a deep reverence in the service and sacrifice of others, such as Mother Theresa or Gandhi as they dedicated themselves to service of the poor and underprivileged. You will be presented with no lack of opportunities throughout your life to recognize and cultivate reverence.

If you develop the potential for reverence, you tend to come to a deeper sense of your own place and importance within the world. Reverence develops a balanced perspective, both of your immense worth as an individual and a sense of place in a much larger world and universe. Reverence helps you to feel a not just a greater sense of self-worth, but a sense of balance among the worth of others around you. You begin to see daily occurrences not as routine, but as a series of small miracles. Things you might have taken for granted or viewed as insignificant may reveal greater depth and meaning.

Greater reverence for that which you find significant develops attitude and perspective that makes you more sensitive, considerate, concerned, thoughtful and engaged in those areas in which you find such meaning. A critical process in your own self-discovery is to find those quiet moments during which you may ponder and recognize a sense of reverence towards those things that you determine to mean the most. The deeper our sense of reverence, the more readily you are able to recognize that which is routine or common and that which holds the hint of the divine.

Capacity for Wisdom: Wisdom is a trait that has been revered through the ages. The ancient psalmists promote wisdom as one of the greatest of human acquisitions. Wisdom is specifically defined as the ability to combine knowledge, insight, judgment and experience and turn it into timely, positive and productive actions in a given situation. Wisdom is the innate understanding you can come to of what is needed in a particular situation when you break it down and analyze it from numerous possible perspectives.

The development of wisdom allows you to combine, compare and contrast these multiple points of view and come to a useful understanding of thought, words and actions that bring the most beneficial results for all concerned. Wisdom can increase and deepen based on the breadth of personal experiences and what has been gleaned and retained from them. Wisdom dictates that as your base of knowledge increases, you become aware of the many possibilities that lie beyond the obvious or above current understanding. You become sensitive to what you know and what you do not yet know.

It is implicit in the nature of wisdom that you seek the best possible results for all concerned in any given situation. As you mature, you come to understand that you live less in a world of absolutes, and more in a world of varying degrees of what can be called right or wrong. While there are times where a clear cut right or wrong answer to a situation may be obvious, there are many more dilemmas where a specific "best" answer is not so clear.

While you may internalize and maintain absolute truths or moral maxims, many of life's situations will create dynamics that require you to identify a solution that lay somewhere in between those absolutes. Wisdom allows you to process the most beneficial course of action from an assortment of possibilities. That you may always be able to pick the "best" course of action is not as important as the processes you must go through to make as informed and effective an assessment as possible.

Even the best and seemingly wisest of actions can meet with failure due to changing or unforeseen circumstances. What is vital is that you store knowledge, experience and judgment to be able to recall and assemble these factors in preparation for the frequent situations that require judgment and action. As with any potential, wisdom is particularly dependent on time and a variety of experiences, both successful and unsuccessful, in its development.

Capacity to Overcome Adversity: There are few days in an ordinary life in which lack some sort of setback or difficulty. Trials and challenges confront you at every turn. Whether it is something as trivial as choosing the slow line in a grocery store to the destruction of an unpredicted natural disaster or the devastation of prematurely losing a loved one, we all face those challenging moments that can shape and define us as an individual. The critical issue is how you will react and what you will do when faced with such pivotal and moving scenarios.

Adversity raises its head in many guises. It has been a popular bent of the philosophers to reflect on the nature and cause of human suffering. The individual that seeks to maximize their potential must, through time and experience, develop strength and form the mindset to overcome adversity whenever it is encountered. You can either shrink from the challenges that adversity brings or view such moments as definitive, allowing the opportunity to deepen and strengthen personal character and resolve.

The personal tests that adversity brings will shape your spiritual determination. They are a test of your personal will to overcome and move forward, not losing sight of those factors that would contribute to your $\Delta Y[a]$. You can use adversity as an excuse not to progress, learn and grow, or you can use it as a springboard to the development of greater strength and will. You will intuitively come to understand your divine nature more deeply through the strength of overcoming adversity. You will be able to more clearly recognize the sources of true joy and dispel sources of true sorrow.

A critical point to remember in developing the potential to overcome adversity is the understanding that you always have the freedom to choose your attitude and actions in the face of any crisis. A positive attitude in the face of great crisis, stress or failure comes from a foundation of faith and confidence that you have control over your own inner self, even if you might not be in complete control of your surrounding circumstances. There is no doubt that frequently in the course of your life you will encounter stumbling blocks that challenge your ability and will to develop your potentials. How you act and react to these situations will directly affect your character and positive future development. Determination, not discouragement, in the face of adversity is a catalyst that enables and supports the development of other key potentials.

The Capacity for Empathy: Empathy is the ability to vicariously experience the thoughts and feelings of others. Developing your potential for empathy is vital to your ability to develop multiple points of view and to understand differing perspectives. Empathy allows you to more closely relate to and learn from others. Empathy is one of the greatest learning processes, enabling you to expand your understanding beyond your own actions through the actions and feelings of others. Developing empathy directly contributes to your library of intuitive knowledge as you learn to feel what others feel and experience what others have experienced. While empathy does not give the same intensity and reality of your own personal experience, it does help to intuitively feel and internalize similar emotions.

Capacity for Faith: Faith is a foundational potential that is a key to the forward momentum of all other potentials. Faith can be defined, in its simplest form, as the belief in your ability to grow, develop and expand in any given area, even if you have no previous experience with that area. You place belief in the yet unseen truth or validity of a particular principle with the hope that acting upon that principle will yield a positive result. Faith in an action is the precursor to properly taking that action.

You must first believe that you might see results of positive actions and behaviors that can develop your potentials before you ever pursue them. As actions yield positive results, your faith is reinforced and you develop additional confidence in that respective potential. Without faith you feel helpless; you lack initiative due to a lack of confidence in any result, thus lacking forward movement. A lack of faith opens the door for fear, doubt and discouragement, all of which can turn the direction of your progress from positive to neutral, or negative. The necessity of belief in your own potentials will be discussed in more detail in Chapter Five.

Capacity for Spiritual Growth: The overall growth and progress of your spiritual or intuitive nature is paramount to the completeness of your being. Like any other potential, whether mental, physical or spiritual, you must measure progress day by day, month by month and year by year. What you must come to understand is that this aspect of your nature has an almost unlimited capacity to grow, expand and progress. As you gather experience and mature you can become ever more attuned to the feelings, impressions and unspoken understandings that imprint themselves spiritually upon you. You are able to gather these cumulative impressions and experiences and use them as a lens to keep subsequent actions and decisions in focus. Over time you will experience a deeper sense of self as well as a deeper and broader understanding of the world around you. You will come to understand new and more far reaching implications in the events of your life.

You will develop a connection with the divine and utilize that dynamic in all that you do. You will assign meaning to your life experiences that have implications beyond the present. As discussed earlier, it is important to envision the spiritual side of yourself as something that has greater form and power than just your physical and biological self. If you assume that a part of you will survive and endure, you must also assume that the educating, nurturing and overall growth of that ongoing part is most important.

Capacity for Change/Repentance: There is always opportunity to change and correct errors and mistakes that would send a potential on a negative down slope. Being imperfect creatures, we are all subject to weaknesses and mistakes. Your primary responsibility to your highest potentials is to recognize and correct mistakes once you realize they have been made. This process of spiritual change, or rededication to correct principle that guides potential, is often called repentance in Judeo-Christian vernacular. It is the powerful process through which you can identify actions or behaviors and have the courage to forsake such behavior if it does not lead you in a positive direction more in line with your $\Delta Y(a)$.

As a dynamic being, change is an inseparable part of your life process. You are always growing and changing. You are either growing in a positive or negative direction. Exercising the capacity to correct your actions, to align your behaviors with those that would contribute to potential rather than detract from it, requires both courage and constant diligence. While change is a constant, enforcing progressive and positive change requires work, commitment and constant dedication. It is not an easy process to continually reach for the positive. What is important is that you understand you have the power to choose that path towards the positive if you are willing to work for it. And when you recognize actions that bring negative value to your potentials, you have the power to choose to correct those actions. The door is always open and the pathway upward is always prepared. Such change is a process you have complete control over as you establish you priority of choice.

Capacity for Forgiveness: A similar and equally important capacity to change and repentance is that of forgiveness. You will always encounter from time to time situations that bring offense or harm. Situations that could infringe upon your ability to grow develop and enjoy life as you choose. As difficult as it might seem at times, it is a powerful potential to be able to forgive those who have contributed to negative situations or given offense and move on.

One of the unfortunate dynamics of human interaction is that those individuals committed to paths and actions of negative potential can drag down others around them. Just as the development of positive potentials can uplift, negative potentials can destroy. It is critical that when you have encountered a negative event that you free yourself from its consequences as quickly as possible. Forgiveness is a tool that helps free you from emotionally negative effect. Without the capacity to forgive and move forward, motives of bitterness resentment or revenge could easily replace more positive mental and spiritual pursuits.

If you have trouble exercising the capacity to forgive, you can become trapped in the negative potential path of others and continually carry the negative effects they have engendered long after the actual events have passed. It is not necessary that the offending parties recognize their errors or seek to recompense those they have offended. If they continue down a negative slope, you must free yourself from that negativity by being able to forgive and proceed forward and upward. The attitude of true forgiveness frees you to move forward on the path of your choosing, neutralizing any negative potential others may seek to impose.

Capacity for Joy and Sorrow: Intrinsic in the human experience are the joys and triumphs of victories and achievement in life, whether small or large. Joy is not always easy to quantify, but as the old saying goes "you know it when you feel it". The capacity to have joy in your own growth and achievements is matched by sharing joy in the positive accomplishments of others. Joy is mainly activated when we can share that joy, although it does serve as a personally lifting experience.

Joy is also closely connected to love, for example when we simply joy in the presence of those closest to us. Joy is always attached to those potentials that uplift, that create positive and upward movement in potential. Joy is a natural outcome of seeing our potentials grow, blossom and fulfill. Joy is magnified when it is shared. When it comes to experiencing joy one with another, one plus one sometimes equals more than two. Joy, taken by itself, is a monument to the importance of the importance of the non-empirical. While joy is virtual immeasurable, would a life be life without joy?

Sorrow, taken as the emotional opposite of joy, is not exclusively a negative emotion. A capacity to sorrow with another implies empathy. It implies a shared understanding and support that is necessary and helpful in times of distress. Equally, sorrow is a fine measure, an internal alarm, to help give insight into the difficulty of negative experiences. While the actions of others, or circumstance itself, may create negative events that trigger sorrow, your ability to channel sorrow as a motivation for positive action and empathy with other is a positive potential.

As you develop the potentials found in your spiritual nature, you will also feed and nurture your mind and body. Ultimately, to reach your greatest personal potential, spiritual growth must be the top priority. It leads the way in all other potential development. It is impossible to have complete health of mind and body without health of the spirit; a health that reaches for and nurtures those positive potentials of which the spirit is capable.

<u>Key Potentials Associated Primarily with the Mind</u>:

The human mind is a deep and complex phenomenon. Modern science has been able to finitely break down areas in the human brain where specific bio-electric activity occurs that is identified as thought, feeling or bodily function. The human mind has often been described as the world's greatest computer; assembling impressions, data and sensory inputs while simultaneously running all of the functions of a living organism. If the human body is a marvel of biological engineering, the human mind is the highlight of the entire structure. As we continue to make strides in identifying those areas of activity in the brain that seem to produce specific activities, the output of all mental activity must still be measured in terms of specific behaviors. Your very words, ideas and behaviors are the products that you produce from the factory of your mind. And as the modern age of technology and information might suggest, the human mind seems to be an almost bottomless well of information and ideas.

We continue to break down barriers of information, science and technology. New discoveries and the boundaries of current knowledge are being pushed regularly. Ten years ago, the genetic therapy being used today was merely a dream. Twenty years ago who would have thought it possible to carry the data now available on a cellular phone. Thirty years ago it would have been difficult to imagine the internet as it is configured today. Sixty years ago space travel was an evolving concept and the idea of putting a man on the moon still seemed far-fetched. Seventy five years ago cures for many of the diseases that are almost extinct today, such as polio, had not crossed anyone's mind. One hundred years ago travelling at or beyond the speed of sound was unimaginable. One hundred and fifty years ago the idea of powered flight was unthinkable. Two hundred years ago the idea of illuminating an entire city with electric lights was a fairy tale. One can only imagine what wonders we might think of next.

The very output resulting from the machinations of the human mind are testament enough of the importance of developing the key positive potentials associated with the mind. Mental development is a life long journey that, barring physical handicap or impairment, can lead you ever upward in a positive direction. As will be discussed further in Chapter 6, the mind is a fabulous engine of ideas and action. You can never really turn off the mind (without chemical or toxic assistance) during your waking hours. The mind is always firing, constantly flowing with ideas and information.

The inner sanctum of the mind can create the most beautiful symphonies, groundbreaking mathematical or chemical formulae, or designs for an award winning building. Conversely, the mind can also generate horror and devastation beyond imagination. The mind can design better and more powerful weapons to destroy, develop political ideas that oppress and enslave or justify philosophies that lead to nothing but sadness and despair. Governed by the intuition and sensitivity of the spirit, the mind can and should be focused on those potentials that will result in productive ideas and positive actions.

As a reminder to the examination of intellectual potential, the direction of the thoughts and the potentials you recognize and develop are strictly up to you. You are free to choose your ideas and actions regardless of environment or circumstance. You cannot always choose the results that your thoughts and actions may lead to, but you are always capable, barring mental impairment, of making your own choices in any situation. True individual freedom and true individual responsibility to activate your inner potentials begins with the simple recognition that the choice to do so is up to you and no one else. In the final measure and analysis of your life you will need to clearly see that thoughts, actions and attitudes are the result of your own choices, deliberate or consequential. The final bill of your cumulative thoughts and actions must be presented to you, and only you, to be paid. The thoughts and ideas that you formulated throughout your life will be yours to own. You cannot attribute them to anyone else but yourself. You always have the freedom to choose to accept or reject any idea or action regardless of the circumstance.

The potentials listed below are the key core potentials that will contribute to the development of the mind. While the numbers of psychological sub-categories that could be categorized within the human mind are numerous, the core potentials discussed here cover the basics needed to move forward in a productive manner. These key capacities describe the fundamental characteristics needed to ascend towards your ultimate intellectual abilities.

Capacity for Intelligence: Your overall intelligence is your ability to logically and creatively process all of the data received through your physical senses as well as your intuitive feelings. The output of this internal processing consists of courses of action, organization of ideas and reactive feelings within a given situation. Traditional definitions try to narrow the parameters of intelligence to define problem solving, language skills or other specific criteria. While the output of intelligence can be tested and measured to some degree to assign it a value relative to others, the core of your intelligence consists of a deeper, less quantifiable essence. Your overall intelligence can be shaped and increased by consistent application of your highest potentials. It consists of a dimension of accumulated knowledge both empirical and intuitive. It is most beneficial to operate under an assumption that your intelligence is free to grow, develop and expand as you choose to nurture it within the parameters of all of your positive potentials.

This definition implies that intelligence is not a fixed quantity. It posits that intelligence has the capacity to grow, change and develop. While your physical makeup and biological limitations have some effect as housing for your intelligence, it is most helpful to view intelligence as an independent and sustainable phenomenon of its own. Just as the physical body can be strengthened by regular exercise, intelligence can be exercised and grown as well. Certain aspects of intellectual growth are certainly measurable. The capacity to solve complex math equations or the ability to master a foreign language can be measured quantifiably. However, much of the intellectual growth that you are capable of is less tangible and measurable. While the scientist might say that if it is immeasurable, it cannot exist, the experience of many great individuals suggests that such growth and expansion is indeed tangible, though not always visible.

For example, how can one measure the ability of certain Native American wise men that seem to be able to measure changes in plant and animal behavior and predict weather phenomenon? How can you measure a surgeon's sudden and unexpected discovery of a new life changing procedure? How can you measure a ground breaking new economic theory that accurately predicts a market's behavior? How is it possible to quantify the ability of a young child to play a musical instrument at a master level? While the fruits of the development of intelligence are often discernible, the process of the growth and expansion of that intelligence usually is not. To envision your highest potential, you must assume that your capacity for intelligence can increase; you must not see intelligence as a fixed and unchangeable asset. You must assume that a constant exercise and nourishment of your intellect will feed that intellect and result in positive growth.

This is not to imply that all levels of intelligence are equally attainable in an individual person over the same time frame. From general observation of a population it is obvious that the degree of intelligence varies from person to person. There are only so many Galileos, Newtons, Mozarts, or Einsteins that come along in a generation. The point you must be aware of is that whatever level of intelligence you are given you are capable through our own choices and diligence of improving upon it. Where there is some, you can develop more. Where there is more, you can improve upon that yet again. Progress in a positive direction, yielding improvement and expansion upon that which you have already obtained, seeking to obtain more, is the dynamic that truly matters. If you believe that intelligence is fixed and unchangeable, you have already conceded the battle for progression and development in this universal potential.

Viewing intelligence as a non-fixed quantity allows you not only to recognize and grow your intellectual capacity, it also implies that intelligence can be absorbed. In other words it is partially transferable. It implies you can obtain intelligence, and the information and ideas that accompany it, from family, friends, associates and colleagues. It implies that you may not only internally absorb ideas or concepts, but you may internalize the intelligence processes behind them to a degree. Picture it as a transfer of energies as well as ideas.

One of the greatest satisfactions in life can be the exchange of ideas and intelligence with those whom you hold dear or look up to with respect. You may realize these exchanges in a personal situation or through the exchange of written or recorded information. There are a great many people of faith that attribute the highest intelligence to God or a Supreme Being. And as you can benefit from greater intelligence than your own, so you should be able to benefit from the highest source of all intelligence. You are rewarded in sharing and absorbing intelligence according to your diligence in seeking to obtain it. And the better and more complete the source of contributors to intelligence, the more you stand to benefit.

Capacity for Learning: Each day of our lives is a learning experience. Each moment of each day you are processing information about what is happening around you. There is so much information available each minute of each day that you can only absorb a small percentage of everything that is available. Your capacity to learn is a cornerstone in conjunction with your capacity for love in shaping your ultimate potential.

It is interesting that you literally cannot turn your mind off during your waking hours. You are constantly bombarded by information via your senses. What you do with that information, in other words what you chose to allow in and process and what you choose to ignore, will ultimately determine who you become. Your ability to learn is as much a product of your choices, desires and attitude as it is about your opportunities. You must choose to learn, it cannot be forced upon you. If you choose to disregard information that can be of use, either through formal conditioning or experience, you are choosing a degree of ignorance over learning. The quality of what you learn is also encompassed in your choices. You can learn volumes of trivial information that may have little practical application or use. You can spend your time in unproductive or mindless entertainment. You can conversely apply your thoughts to information that has benefit both to yourself and others.

There are so many varied channels through which you are able to learn. Much research has been compiled identifying the differences between auditory, visual and tactile learning. A majority of learning may be attributed to the senses you must not discount intuition and imagination. However you best come to learn, your greatest potentials revolve around your ability to process and internalize a huge variety of information and emotion. That you have the capacity to do so, and do so in a progressive and ever increasing manner is what must be recognized. The patterns of your learning, and the selections of what learning you decide will be relevant, will play a most significant role in the progression of your intellect and character.

If our personal assumptions shape anything significantly, perhaps our capacity to learn is shaped most thoroughly by the sets of assumptions we operate under. Those assumptions are changeable and fluid, yet they color every impression we obtain from the world around us. The assumptions outlined in the Salvation Equation apply directly to the learning process. The Salvation Equation posits that the assumptions internalized in these pages are the most useful in extending accurate and productive learning insofar as it applies to personal development. The assumptions in this book lend to the highest slope of your $\Delta Y[a]$ as you continue on the learning curve of life's experiences.

The human mind can be compared favorably to a computer. The usefulness of the output is solely dependent on the quality of the input; garbage in-garbage out. As with a computer, your potential in learning is dependent on the quality of information and experience you obtain, and the veracity of the lens of assumptions you process it through. However, unlike a computer, you have the ability to develop filters to sort through and sift out information you decide is useless. Your processing, both empirical and intuitive, in conjunction with your ability to freely choose, gives you the unique power to shape the path of your own learning. You are free to sculpt whatever form you choose out of the raw material of information encountered.

Capacity for Empirical Knowledge: Hand in hand with the expansion of your intelligence is the development of your personal library of empirical knowledge. This body of knowledge consists of facts and phenomenon as they are able to be observed and measured. Most major developments in science, engineering, medicine, finance, or economics have been the result of continual accumulation of specific empirical knowledge. Your capacity to analyze, understand and retain facts and methodologies give you a firmer grasp on the workings of the world around you. Empirical knowledge helps define life processes, the world in which you live and the phenomenon you experience in concrete and re-occurring terms.

As you grow in empirical knowledge you must keep in mind that empirical knowledge is not always absolute. Most measurable occurrences are defined by principles that are developed through the occurrences themselves. These principles or laws may be absolute, or they may eventually be superseded by newer or higher discoveries. We must always keep in mind that empirical knowledge can change over time, and we must be willing to adapt to new ideas and new theories or principles.

Capacity for Logic: Logic is a specific capacity of intellect to organize and see an interrelation between a series of facts and events. When you exercise logic, you focus on reasoning and outcome independent of how you might feel about the situation. You organize facts as they occur and through analysis come to the most obvious or efficient conclusion. The importance of this key potential is the ability to be distanced emotionally from a situation and draw conclusions based solely on the facts. Highly developed logic is necessary to function effectively in highly technical work or in situations that require rapid and accurate analysis. Emotion is engaged only when value needs to be given to the conclusions drawn from logic.

Capacity for Imagination/Creativity/Innovation: You have often heard the mantra that you are only limited by the boundaries of your own imagination. A broad sweeping review of significant moments in world history would reveal a fair representation of the imaginations of a multitude of individuals put into action. There are plenty of examples of the futile and misdirected exercise of imagination, such as the Tower of Babel. There are far more instances where imagination and visualization turned into quantifiable concrete action, such as the invention of the light bulb or the Apollo program that eventually landed a man on the moon.

Where imagination and creativity meet intuitive and empirical knowledge, literal miracles in human achievement may result. There has not been one great work of fictional writing, one great animated feature, one great scientific innovation that did not begin with the seed of creativity and imagination in someone's fertile mind. There is little we can do as human beings or that we have done that does not begin as a flash of inspiration that is creatively developed within the imagination of the mind. Your ability to suddenly recognize and visualize that which was previously unknown or unimagined is one of the great miracles in life.

You truly have an unlimited capacity to imagine. You can visualize almost any possibility, scenario or circumstance within a fertile imagination. Turning such imagination into a reality comes through the process of innovation, which is the ability to concretely bring new ideas and new associations into existence. The beginning of innovation occurs within your imagination.

Innovation itself is both part of the process of our imaginative capacity and the end product in terms of new creations of ideas, systems, processes and products.

While the process of visualizing a real action or circumstance from a universe of innumerable possibilities may be overwhelming to some, it is a life-giving, life-confirming process to others. You have the ability to utilize and develop this three step process. You have the capacity to use your imagination to envision new ideas or concepts, visualize how such new ideas might become a reality and then use your creative potential to make that idea into a ground-breaking reality.

Imagination has the ability to be a constant source of energizing, inspiring, uplifting and confirming activity. This is a critical source of personal becoming as you are able to imaginatively tap a wealth of unseen possibilities; to visualize scenarios of what could be and to create mental priorities regarding specific outcomes you might desire. Conversely, some of the greatest horrors you might ever foresee can be conjured in the imagination. War, rape, murder, theft, conspiracy and even the unthinkable crime of genocide began in the seeds of badly misdirected imaginations. If the positive vector of any potential is most crucial, it is that of imagination. The truism "as a man thinketh so is he" has never been more applicable than in the fertile ground of the human imagination. If we could view the imagination as the stage upon which ideas play out their drama for our personal consideration, we should always exercise caution that no bad actors are allowed to stay on that stage for long.

The innate value to others of what you bring to light within your imagination is also significant. You can entertain powerful possibilities that bring forth new ideas, new science, new medicine, new technology or something as fun and interesting, such as the first feature length cartoon. You can also spend time imagining the trivial, fruitless and wasteful, such as entertaining demeaning gossip, worrying about being kidnapped by aliens or seeing yourself becoming emperor of the world. While it is difficult to say that any particular activity that develops your imagination is harmful, you must be aware and apply this potential in a strictly positive manner to engender positive results.

Capacity for Leadership: The ability to embark upon paths of accomplishment, and the ability to inspire others to follow in a positive direction, is a potential that is widely admired in almost any culture or society. While every individual will inevitably have some opportunity to demonstrate leadership, the exercise of leadership is a potential that many individuals seem reluctant to develop. Memorable events in history often involve an individual or group of individuals that have exercised unusual leadership and brought forth action or change to the world around them. The most notable leaders tend to be political, social or military, where their skills have been acted out on a grand stage, shaping the history of peoples and nations. Julius Caesar, Alexander the Great, King David, Joan of Arc, Christopher Columbus, George Washington, Gandhi, General Eisenhower and so many others all exhibited leadership on a grand scale when given an even grander world stage. But many individual's potential for leadership is frequently exercised on a far less ostentatious scale. In most daily interactions, the truest forms of leadership are exercised by simply setting a positive example. Whether you are the most studious student in a science class, the most diligent office worker, the most sensitive and engaged social worker, the most driven athlete, or the most concerned and focused executive, you have the opportunity to exercise leadership by showing examples of what it means to reach for and develop your potential in any given endeavor.

The essence of positive and ethical leadership is being able to identify and do the right things at the right times for the right reasons. The development of positive leadership requires positive potentials in intelligence, knowledge and empathy. Leadership requires an understanding and analysis of a situation combined with the determination to take actions that lead to a desired outcome. It is also the ability to inspire others to believe and follow the path that leads to that positive outcome.

True leadership identifies and contributes to the activation of potentials in others, pointing the direction by word and deed towards which those potentials may be exercised. As with any potential, leadership needs to be focused on positive outcomes. As you activate your leadership potential, by nature you inspire others to follow, or at least to see the vision your leadership provides. If that path or vision is appealing but harmful, as many instances of self-ingratiating or self-indulgent leadership historically have been, you become equally liable for not only your own negative potential, but the negative potentials of others who have chosen to follow that negative lead.

Capacity to determine Attitude: If you ponder the highest applications of personal freedom of thought, you can identify the catalyst of all potentials through the attitudes you choose to adopt. Your attitude is the cumulative applied thought, learning, feeling, reaction and response to a given situation or set of circumstances. You alone have the capacity to freely choose how a specific life situation will affect you. You can determine your own enthusiasm or indifference; your own ardor or hatred; your own hope or discouragement; your own joy or sadness. Your attitude, more than any other component of your psyche, will uniquely determine the slope and ultimate altitude of any and all other positive potentials.

You can determine whether or not you will act upon life situations or be acted upon. While you always have the opportunity to take away learning and experience from any given event, you have the power through the shaping of your attitudes to determine whether that learning and experience will be used for your benefit or to your detriment. In almost any circumstance, even some of the cruelest and most inhumane imaginable, there lies within you the power to glean positive lessons from that circumstance through the shaping of attitude. Even if you learn only perseverance and forgiveness through the worst suffering, you still have the freedom to dignify yourself and others with an attitude that always looks for the positive.

We all know those endearing individuals that maintain a positive attitude. They are frequently seen as an inspirational friend, leader and confidant that spend their time engaged in lifting others. Attitude can be infectious. As one person sees the positive in a given situation, others around them have that perspective opened to them also. The same can be said regarding negative attitudes. If you are around someone who is "on a downer" you may be adversely impacted as well. The truism "attitude equals altitude" could not be more accurate than in the process of activating our potentials. Your attitude is and will always remain a primary determinant in the upward progress towards your ultimate potential.

Capacity to Endure Adversity or Suffering: One potential that truly utilizes the most intense application of attitude is the capacity to endure adverse forms of suffering, physical, spiritual or mental. The deepest nature of your individual character can often be both forged and revealed in the furnace of affliction. Everyone will face tests of endurance through adversity at some point. Whether you are in the midst of serious conflict, subject to disease and illness, deprived of the basic necessities of life, or have fallen short of a highly prized goal in life, you must learn to endure, persevere and to continue to move forward and upward. You will at some point in your life be subject to physical pain or discomfort. You will experience mental anguish and disappointment. You will be subject to or have those around you experience illness and death. How you react, learn and grow from these often transitional experiences plays a huge role in the future direction of your character and potentials.

As many of the great philosophers have pointed out, it is not whether you avoid suffering; it is how you endure the process and how you emerge from adversity with the shaping, confirmation and renewal of your character. The perspective of human life as a process of only enduring suffering is incomplete. You are meant to have both moments of joy and moments of tribulation. It is in the opposition of experiences, stretching your thoughts, skills and emotions to either end of the continuum, that you develop the depth and breadth of your potentials. When you learn to endure through difficult situations and find positive and enlightening lessons from the process, you open the possibilities of other positive potentials that will be realized in a calmer environment. Great personal strength, the kind of strength that forges character in the greatest of potentials, is found in conquering adversity.

Capacity for Sympathy: Closely related to empathy, sympathy is the capacity to relate to the concerns, needs, distresses or other difficult emotional states of another. While empathy implies we can share that emotional state, sympathy is the intellectual and experiential understanding of another's situation. Developing the capacity for sympathy elevates the internalizing and understanding of your own priorities and enables you to evaluate and respond to the needs of others. Sympathy with others provides a connection to their situation, their needs and their feelings and allows you to utilize your potential for wisdom, comfort and service on their behalf.

One of our primary responsibilities as human beings is to lift each other and comfort each other in times of need. Only through the sensitive development of sympathy can you forge an intimate connection to another's needs or struggles and respond in kind with appropriate service. As you respond to the needs of others in sympathy, you strengthen your own catalog of intuitive knowledge and emotional learning through the vicarious experiences of others. In the process of sympathizing, you can give of yourself in response to the needs of others, but you can also receive in the shared insights such experiences give.

Capacity for Service: A cornerstone of interrelationships and the root of opportunity to learn with each other and grow from each other are realized in the capacity for service. Service is putting the immediate needs of another ahead of your own personal priorities. Service is lending understanding, comfort and whatever helping hand is needed at a given moment. Your capacity and your mindset towards service will heavily influence the direction and slope of your other potentials involving relationships. Selflessness and service with an unrestricted desire to see others around you reach their highest potential is a critical facet in attaining your own potential.

You are never truly alone in the world, and the most important asset we have is each other. That is, if we approach each other with the mindset of service.

Love is defined for the purpose of potential as the conscious choice to put the ability of another to become and reach their highest potential equal to or ahead of your own. In this light, service is the outward manifestation of the inner motivation that such love provides. Service is the bridge that crosses between the spiritual manifestations of love and the physical acts of caring for one another. If you truly care for another, you will seek to serve, lift and better them. Through this process you will discover that service is the straightest and quickest path to bettering yourself. This principle is universal, and it consistently bears fruit with conscientious application.

It has been often said that if you are not feeling good about yourself, or are struggling with some aspect of your life, in other words if you are struggling to reach your potential, forget yourself and find a way to lift and serve someone else. If you diligently find such opportunities, your cares soon fade and we find yourself anxiously engaged in activities that lift and inspire everyone involved. Your capacity for service, and the love of others that motivates such service, are a special key to the positive development of character and potential.

<u>Key Potentials Associated Primarily with the Body</u>:

The human body is a marvel of biological engineering. The complex systems, structures and designs that comprise our physical body are a miraculous creation. The manners in which the body maintains itself and repairs itself are equally marvelous. The body has been carefully studied since the dawn of mankind. It is only in the last few centuries that we have made any real serious scientific progress in cataloging, identifying and understanding the incredible complexity and interrelationships of our physical and biological systems. And there is much yet to discover as the recent foundations of biological and medical discovery are advanced. However you choose to care and maintain your physical body, you should nurture a perspective of admiration and respect for the marvel it is.

Among all of the physical creations on this planet, the human body stands out uniquely for both its level of sophistication, variety and its fragility within our ecosystem. While many creatures have adapted physical traits that enable them to adjust to their environments more effectively, the human body remains fairly consistent throughout the various climates and cultures of the world. We have to create physical adaptations through use of our intelligence and other potentials to shape our environment and, where necessary, overcome it.

While there is a wide variety of appearances and unique physical consistencies throughout the world based on race and genetic adaptations within various subcultures, the physical makeup of all humans is essentially the same. Barring congenital problems, we all have two eyes to see with, two ears, two hands, nose, shoulders, stomach, heart, knees, etc. We are all essentially equipped with the same tools with which to experience the world. We all start off from roughly the same point when it comes to physical experiences. While various cultures and differing environments may provide a much different variety of physical experiences, both exalting and challenging, we have a fairly level playing field with which to work and move forward.

However, the pace at which we are able to move forward physically is determined by more than our will.

Another aspect of the physical is that we all inherit our physical traits through the genetic combinations we receive from our parents. We are essentially stuck with this formula for our entire lives. In essence, we have to "play the hand we are dealt." For example, a person with a light frame and slender white, slow-twitch muscle should probably not seek a career in Olympic power lifting. A large-framed man with heavy dense red fast-twitch muscle fiber will have a difficult time competing in a marathon. Despite the variation within the essential structure of the human body, you do have the ability to discover and make the best use of those physical traits that you have been given. Whether you have the propensity to be a sprinter or a distance runner, whether you are naturally strong or very coordinated, whether you can hold your breath for a long time or hold a difficult yoga position, you are gifted with physical capabilities that we can develop, share and enjoy.

The body is also the housing for the mind and the spirit. While extreme physical achievements are not necessary for developing capacities of mind and spirit, a balance between the interrelationships of each is important. To achieve our highest potentials the synergies between mind, spirit and body need to be maximized. Neglect of our bodies is reflected in diminished mental function. Spiritual pain can often be reflected through physical symptoms. Strength in each area as well as discipline in each area results in the most prolific potentials in each area.

There are many instances when the body has experienced handicaps to one degree or another that may inhibit normal function and may prohibit certain physical activity. It is notable in many such instances that the mind and spirit can often help compensate for physical hindrances. It is a testament to the delicate interrelationship of the mind, body and spirit that individuals that experience such challenges often find ways to compensate and overcome. It is ultimately up to your spirit to exercise final control over both your mind and your body. It is through the ultimate discipline of the spirit that requisite discipline of the mind and body are realized (as has been demonstrated through the ancient practices of Chi Gong and other artful disciplines between the spiritual and physical). Even with physical difficulties, you can progress in your quest for your highest potentials.

Capacity for Physical Strength and Endurance: Our bodies begin to grow and become stronger literally from the day we are born. The physical configurations of bones, joints and ligaments as well as muscle type and ultimate muscle mass determine the outright potential for developing physical strength and endurance. The size and capacity of your heart and lungs also determine your ultimate threshold of physical activity. You cannot control these genetic factors to any large degree. What you can do is create disciplines that exercise the body consistently to develop strength and stamina.

Developing and maintaining these traits gives confidence in your ability to perform basic physical or more complicated athletic tasks. The daily necessity of disciplined exercise that develops strength and endurance also develops mental and spiritual discipline. If you care for your body and its condition you will seek ways to move and strengthen your body regularly. You will choose those things you eat and drink and otherwise ingest carefully. You will tend to avoid anything that might do harm to the body, creating the soundest possible environment for your mind and spirit. An efficient and well-functioning body creates a pathway for the freest intellectual and spiritual activities.

Capacity for Physical Perception: Much of what you understand about the world around you comes from input you have received through your physical senses. Sight, sound, smell, taste and touch are the reception points of the majority of experiences in the physical world. Your capacity to experience and interpret these inputs will certainly become more diverse over time as physical experiences become more varied. You feel physical elation as well as fatigue. You hear sounds that are pleasant as well as annoying. You taste foods that are delicious and things that are nauseating. Your physical perceptions shape your views of the realities around you. Your physical perceptions can be sharpened over time but are, much like physical conditioning, subject to the genetic and biological limitations you were born with. In other words, there is only so far you can refine your senses. But refined they may be to an extent.

For purposes of striving for your highest potentials, the intuitive input you receive, those impressions not necessarily born out of input from the physical senses, should be weighted carefully as well. The most obvious realities in daily life are communicated through our physical perceptions. But the deeper realities, the more enduring and divine nature of self, can often lie outside the realm of these fundamental perceptions of the physical senses. You have a responsibility to your own ultimate potential to balance and seek understanding of the interplay and importance between these realms of perception. Time, experience, patience and careful thought and reflection are the tools necessary to integrate these diverse inputs.

Capacity for Healing: The body has a remarkable ability to heal itself when exhausted or injured. The field of healing has seen progressive and interesting new breakthroughs in recent decades. Philosophies that emphasize spiritual or mental healing frameworks and techniques are gaining credibility in the face of ever more detailed clinical approaches. The fields of medicine and nutrition also continue to progress with more research as well as anecdotal data. The majority of the body's healing occurs with rest. Proper sleep and nutrition are critical for healing from either injury or overwork.

For the purpose of your potential, you can control your body's capacity to heal in so far as it is able through proper nutrition, rest, rehabilitation and positive mental attitude. Keeping your body, healthy, fit, rested and properly recovered are all essential to maximizing the potentials that flow through the mind and spirit via proper physical function.

Capacity for Robust Health: Proper care for the body, following established and tried principles of health and nutrition, result in the ability to function physically on a level that allows potentials of the mind and spirit to flourish. Science is always discovering new inroads to human health. There are constantly new inroads to the biology, chemistry and functionality of the body itself. By your own experimentation, study and application of known principles of good health, you should be able to maintain good balance throughout your life. External factors such as unexpected disease, environmental toxicity or congenital weaknesses can always influence the path to increased health. Nevertheless, you have the freedom to choose how to nourish and strengthen your body under ordinary circumstances.

Even the best efforts to maintain good health must eventually fail. Your body, like all physical matter, is subject to entropy (the eventual breakdown and disassociation of all organized molecular systems). There will be a point, despite your best efforts to nourish and strengthen your body, when entropy will start to take over. At a certain age, determined by both genetics and personal health habits, your body will start to deteriorate. This deterioration occurs at a cellular level. The body cannot renew individual cells at a rate equal to individual cell mortality. Over decades this deterioration, even with the most stringent efforts at maintaining health, will result in the complete failure of physical systems and death. The highest application of your physical potentials is to slow the pace of entropy. You cannot ultimately stop it.

This phenomenon emphasizes the fact that physical potentials are temporary. While you should regard your body and health as something precious and marvelous, ultimately the most important function of the body is to provide a well-functioning tabernacle for the spirit. Allowing the divine potentials of the spirit to be nurtured and developed through the vehicle of the mind within the operational jurisdiction of the body defines our cumulative mortal existence.

The potentials of each of these components are interdependent. They each require consistent attention and nurturing. They are each synergistic with the others. Positive effect in one area leads to positive opportunities in the others. Negative outcomes in one area create negative possibilities in the others. By looking at yourself in terms of these three uniquely intertwined facets, you will more effectively identify, activate and develop your highest potentials for each.

Epilogue: The Laws of Conservation of Energy and Conservation of Matter

If we view a human being as an organized system, consisting of biological matter and energy, which may encompass activity of the mind and spirit, is there a scientific rationale that would support the idea of the divine or eternal nature of man? Actually there is, in the basic laws of empirical physics that describe the law of conservation and matter (or mass).

In physics, the law of Conservation of Energy states that the total energy of an isolated system remains constant, it is said to be conserved over time. This law means that energy can neither be created nor destroyed; rather, it can only be transformed from one form to another. The law implies that mass can neither be created nor destroyed, although it may be rearranged in space, or the entities associated with it may be changed in form. The law of conservation of matter, or mass, or principle of mass conservation states that for any system closed to all transfers of matter and energy, the mass of the system must remain constant over time, as system's mass cannot change, so quantity cannot be added nor removed. Hence, the quantity of mass is conserved over time. (Richard Feynman (1970). The Feynman Lectures on Physics Vol I. Addison Wesley.)

If we accept these laws as absolutes, we must also accept the fact that upon death a human being cannot lose energy or mass, it must simply be transformed. Transformed into what. If you accept a human being as a closed system of biological function, then the inquiry ends there. All matter and energy is transformed into decaying biological compost. But we do not seem to be closed systems. We take in food and water put out work, energy, thoughts, desires and so forth. If we work under the assumption of an open system, the argument can be made that every watt of the energy contained in an individual must be somehow transformed upon the collapse of the material support system. It must, in fact, be preserved. But transformed into what?

Here we enter the realm of philosophy and religion. But the main point is, if we assume a transformation, we must assume some sort of continuation. It makes equal sense under the reading of the laws, and is by far the more productive and optimistic assumption under which to operate.

Chapter 5

<u>The Fundamental Necessity of Faith in Your Own Ultimate Potential</u>

The journey to the highest realization of your potentials begins with the kernel of belief in your own ability to learn, grow and become. It is difficult to point yourself in a direction that consistently raises your potentials and realizes progressive personal growth without the underlying fundamental belief that you are able to do so. Belief in yourself and faith in the underlying principles that enable you to obtain your potential are the first and primary ingredients in a daily recipe for action that results in positive growth.

Such faith is a principle of action. You can accomplish nothing without first having some level of faith that your actions would bring a specific and desired result. Even if the results of your actions do not turn out to be what you had envisioned, you at least began with some idea of an outcome, realistic or not, completely understood or not, before you acted. Faith is a personal hope or desire that a principle you have not yet perfected and internalized has real merit and value. Even if you have little or no experience with something, you can exercise faith that there is a real dimension or truth to that specific something. This level of faith drives you to actions based on belief that the underlying principle will yield the results you desire.

It requires a degree of personal faith to understand and internalize the six divine assumptions outlined in Chapter 2. It requires further faith to act upon these assumptions and seek positive results from those actions. It requires faith in the principles of your ultimate potentials, believing they are a part of you and that with proper actions you can slowly and surely fulfill them. The consistent application of faith, in both yourself and the unrealized principles that guide and fulfill your potentials, must be exercised again and again. Over time, if you have placed your faith in a correct principle, in a principle that does indeed yield results in the fulfillment of your potential, you will begin to understand, apply and internalize the principle based on those positive results.

 For example, if you exercise faith that if you begin to jog five days a week that you will lose weight, increase your cardiovascular capacity, and eventually watch your time per mile decrease, your actions will tend to support the outcomes you have envisioned. After several months of jogging, if you begin to see a drop in weight, if your body's stamina is elevated and if your mile times are shorter, your faith is strengthened and renewed as you gain knowledge of the principles behind your actions.

If you continue to exercise faith over time in a true or correct principle, there will come a time when the exercise of that faith has been fulfilled with knowledge of that principle. In our example, if after many months of jogging you have realized all of the outcomes you exercised faith in, and are enjoying running in local club road races, you no longer just exercise faith in the benefits of jogging. You know what jogging has done for you. You will know that others may reap similar benefits from jogging. Your faith has been confirmed and transformed into knowledge of the principle. Your potential for physical stamina and strength is likewise being confirmed by undertaking actions that correctly and accurately fulfill that potential.

Faith, Action, Result, Greater Faith to Action Spiral

And so it is with each potential that you identify and choose to activate. You must first exercise a belief that you can do something to nurture that specific potential. You will then move forward, taking actions that tend to support that potential. As you find your abilities increased with time and effort, you confirm the truth of the potential and, with continued application, internalize it. You move onward and upward, reinforcing the positives that you have achieved. This is the fundamental pathway of all human achievement. Believe first and then act accordingly. With consistent results from your actions the principle of faith is transformed into a principle of knowledge and understanding. If you have faith in correct principles, you will harvest the results of profitable, well-directed actions.

Your personal ability and power to become whatever you envision is directly linked to the strength of your faith. Faith is the power behind all coherent action. Without faith you may lack productive direction in your life. You must believe first and foremost in your own ability to learn, act and grow. You must also believe that there exist specific actions that will bring certain results. These beliefs then encourage you to search out and recognize the principles behind those actions and results. The more consistently you internalize the underlying principles that give strength and guidance to your faith, the more empowered you are to act. The more empowered you are to act the larger your influence upon yourself and the world around you. If you have internalized and acted upon correct principles, your actions will result in greater benefit to you and all those whom you have influenced. Faith enlarges the footprints you leave throughout the cumulative series of actions that comprise your life.

But it is critical that your faith be directed toward true, accurate and correct principles to achieve positive results. Faith in false, inaccurate or useless principles will bring unproductive results and will not reinforce your potentials. For example, there is always the stereotype of the doomsayer standing on the street corner with a sign proclaiming the world will end on a certain date. In fact, there have been individuals and institutions that have built a following on such claims. These individuals truly exercised faith in the idea that the world would end. When the world did not end on the appointed date, their faith was confirmed false and knowledge of things as they currently are was restored.

In the middle ages, the prevailing scientific model of the earth was that it was flat, and that if one traveled far enough they would eventually fall off the edge into an abyss. Even though the idea of a round earth was explored by the Greeks as early as the sixth century, when Columbus sailed in the late 1400s many truly believed it was blasphemous to consider a round earth and

Columbus would never be seen again. Today, such a belief has been refuted many times over by actual experience in travelling across a round globe. We can now obtain solid evidence of the truth of a round earth through pictures of the planet taken from space. The false belief in a flat earth was gradually replaced by a belief in a round earth which inspired exploration and eventual confirmation through experience. And so it is with every principle of faith that governs our potentials. If the principle upon which we believe and then act is true and correct, we will eventually come to an innate understanding that the results of actions based on that principle generate. Faith in incorrect principles will inevitably lead to a series of misplaced efforts and dead ends.

This is the core of the power of the principle of faith. If faith is placed in that which, though currently perhaps unseen, unknown or unfamiliar, has actual merit based in truth and reality, that faith will eventually yield correct actions which will consistently produce positive results. As stated earlier, the first place to place your faith is in yourself. This means to place faith in both the self that you can now experiment with and come to know through life experience, considering that time, work and practice will grant you an increase in potential if you manage the process well. It also means placing faith in the intuitive side of you that remains yet to be discovered and developed.

It suggests that placing faith in a divine potential, though yet not fully known or discovered, may become part of who you are as you progress in developing all possible potentials. It requires faith that this yet undiscovered nature exists and can become real. Further, it requires faith in power and intelligence beyond the self that can be ever present and assist in the process of growth of self, both practical and divine. The six divine assumptions must become subjects of that faith, relying on the reality of the process that the unknown may eventually become known through time and experience.

As stated earlier, faith is the foundational principle of any action. But faith certainly does not preclude the necessity of that action. Faith requires work, effort and application in the positive direction of whatever potentials you chose to activate and nurture. It is the old and ever debated faith-works conundrum. One individual says "I have faith", and that alone secures my well-being. Another states that "faith without works leads to nothing", thus faith in and of itself has no merit. Both are necessary and each relies on the other.

True faith, on its own merits, will eventually motivate to a course of action. Those actions, if founded in faith of potential realities, will produce works that bear fruit and get results. Consistent results both increase faith and form the basis for knowledge of any given principle and potential. Thus both faith and action are required. Faith in and of itself is critical to begin moving forward. True faith leads to true action. Actions based on well-placed faith are just as critical. Where one is, there eventually will you find the other.

Chapter 6

We are Always, Thinking, Choosing and Becoming…Something

<u>The Process of Becoming is a Permanent Part of our Nature</u>:

The principle of becoming is an inescapable dynamic of human existence. Within the landscape of growth, potential and the dynamics of being human, there is no neutral ground. You are always engaged in becoming, whether you do so consciously or not. In every waking and conscious moment of your existence you are thinking and processing. You are taking in information around you, either through your senses and the empirical data you receive, or through your intuitive senses and spiritual perceptions that you feel. You constantly have to process thoughts and make decisions on what to think, choose and do from moment to moment. There is no off switch as long as one is awake, healthy and active. The central issue to this principle is posited "what are you thinking about and how does that affect what are you becoming".

There is always direction or vector to the idea of becoming. We are either trending upward in what we seek to become, or we are trending downward and away from a potential that may have the opportunity to define us. In your daily activities you must continually make a series of choices. Some are relatively minor or perfunctory, such as choosing the spoon with which to eat breakfast cereal. Others are more complex, such as a calculated reaction to a co-worker's request that you consider unreasonable. But each decision you make leads to another decision and another after that and so on. It becomes critical to establish a positive vector to each minute decision that bears any importance to your potentials to ensure that you are becoming empowered in the potentials that you seek. Every decision must be rooted in the pursuit of higher potential to maintain a positive direction or vector to the actions that follow.

Because the principle of becoming is innate and permanent in the very make-up of a human being, you cannot escape the consequences of your choices in relation to becoming. In other words, there is nowhere to hide from the dynamic of becoming. It is active whether you like it or not, whether you choose to recognize it or not and whether you understand it or not. For these reasons you should be ever aware of the principle of becoming and how your everyday thoughts and choices affect that becoming. The old proverb "as a man thinketh so is he" has broad relevance to the dynamic of becoming.

Each decision you make and each thought of any significance will have an impact on your becoming. You are either becoming more learned and informed or more ignorant. You are either learning to love or becoming more indifferent. You are either becoming more filled with faith or more given to despair. You are either becoming more physically strong and vigorous or growing weaker and more tired. You are either learning to forgive or harboring resentment. You are either learning to empathize with others or becoming more detached. You are either discerning the truth of yourself or ignoring the deeper potentials within you. There is always the constant pressure of becoming. It is a force that is always being applied to the forging of your character, to the very essence of the self that you have the possibility to grow into.

If the ultimate potentials associated with our constant becoming were truly understood, it would be so far beyond our current perceived limits it would hard to comprehend. To imply that your highest potentials are divine in nature is to imply that the most consistent application of the principle of becoming will naturally direct you toward fulfilling and maximizing those divine potentials.

<u>Three Progressive Life Phases and Orientations of Becoming, Perspective and Self:</u>

Each person throughout their life, if permitted to live for a reasonable period of time, must pass through three distinct and progressive phases of orientation towards themselves, the world they live in and their potentials. These phases are interrelated and progress from one phase to the next is not always smooth or final. As your perspective matures and shifts from one orientation to another, the details and perspectives on life will shift and change also as you see familiar events or situations in the light of increased experience and understanding.

Each phase is defined by your specific focus at that particular time in life. The process of maturation involves developing and refining our dominant focus at any given point in time. In younger years, time is occupied just trying to orient oneself to the complexities of the world we live in. No matter how brilliant, no one can become expert at everything. There is simply too much to take in. Even our best efforts yield competencies at a few things with a great ignorance of many, many others. If you are ever to activate the highest potentials within, you must eventually progress through all three phases to arrive at a state of transcendence over the trappings of the purely material world. The fact is simply that without an initial embrace and

pg. 151

then eventual study and understanding of the metaphysical, not every possible potential can be obtained.

We will label these phases as Formative Orientation, Functional Ascendance and Transcendent Transition. The general nature and dynamics of each phase will be outlined below.

<u>Formative Orientation</u>

From the time of your birth until emergence into adulthood, approximately age twenty five or thirty, is a phase of life labeled as the Formative Orientation. You are born with no memory or thought of any previous existence. The philosophical discussion of whether life begins at conception or birth, or whether your intelligence existed in knowable form prior to birth is beyond the scope of this discussion. Suffice to say that you are an intelligent and sentient being from the day you are born. You come into this world with a clean slate in an infant body with the tools and potentials in embryo that you will need to navigate the winding course of life.

From the first day of your birth you are dependent on others to help you survive and grow. Your first lessons as to who you are, where you are and what your life means will likely come from your parents or other close caregivers. As you grow rapidly in both physical and mental abilities through your early years, your orientation is almost completely on the nature of the physical world around you. You are learning to crawl, then walk, then run. You learn other more advanced skills such as how to swim or throw and catch a ball. You assess the value of physical things around you and seek to give them place and order in your life. You learn which foods taste good and which do not. Sights, smells sounds, everything that can be perceived through the physical senses are new and need to be cataloged as you form your perceptions of self-based value upon your orientation to the physical world.

As you progress through your educational years you begin to learn more advanced orientations. Social bonding, friendships, extended family associations, educational opportunities and relationships all take on relevance and meaning. If you have ambition and opportunity, ideas of career and earning potential form during these years. You envision the physical world and the physical rewards it offers as the innermost nexus of purpose.

The established institutions and cultural touch points are arranged to help you find place, meaning and purpose within this physical world. The ideas and values of what it means to become a productive family member, student, employee or citizen are almost universally taught and propagated based on your cultural orientation as previous generations have understood it, and successfully navigated through it. Thoughts of your own mortality or deeper sense of purpose are most often subordinated during this phase of life, as the requirements of education, accumulation of basic knowledge and acquisition of skill necessary to navigate this new existence occupy the majority of your time and thoughts.

The world is a large and complex place and it requires significant effort on your part not only to become oriented to its many demands but to try and develop a model of understanding that will help you successfully navigate the many pitfalls life might throw in front of you. It is both demanding in terms of time and effort, and most cultures reward the most diligent among us most directly. In other words, your highest efforts are involved in the ideals and definitions of a "productive" member of your culture or society, along with all of the perceived benefits and rewards that may accompany those ideals.

Functional Ascendance

At some point you will have accumulated enough experience and education to feel well oriented and functional in the world as you have come to understand it. You will have accumulated knowledge from family, friends, education and your environment. For many individuals, from roughly age 30 on up through your fifties or sixties you labor to secure the best possible situation in the world as opportunities are made or present themselves. This is a time of careerism and development of more complex relationships. Perhaps work, marriage, family, community oriented positions of service or recognition, advanced or exclusive social groups take on greater relevance. You define your sense of self around confirming roles as they become functional and useful in the economic and social world available to you. The rewards of the advancing ability to manage and profit from the economic and social systems around you become significant and a primary goal of your daily thought and activity.

You discover it is the tendency of the natural economic world that, at whatever level of opportunity is available, to succeed you must dedicate significant amounts of time, effort, study and work to navigate the complex possibilities and advance in prosperity and status. The role models that are presented are often those individuals who have achieved a significant level of fame, power, wealth or achievement within a familiar economic paradigm. These examples are held up and admired as a model for renewed effort towards concepts of success. This is a period of time when the ambitious among us are determined to conquer the world and carve out their piece of the "economic dream" as it is defined for them.

During this period, the many responsibilities associated with advanced relationships and work and social situations have a potential refining effect on your character. You must learn to manage a diverse range of ideas, personalities and situations to both survive and succeed. All of this experience brings unlimited possibilities for maturation and growth. The intellectual and operative functional skills that can enhance your effectiveness in work and value to society remain a priority and point the way towards your best chances for success.

This is also a period of life when most people often enter into a nuclear family relationship of their own. A balance between personal ambitions and goals and the needs of spouse, children and other dependent relationships must take a priority position in your life. Many sociologist call this period of life "the crowded years", attributable to the simple fact there are often not enough hours in a day to meet all of the demands you may face as you attempt to ascend the rungs of family life, work demands and societal opportunity.

<u>Transcendent Transition</u>

At some point along the time line of life, a transition begins to take place. The age and period of life varies widely between individuals based on cultural, religious and personal factors. There should come a point in everyone's lives where the ambitions of economic life and progress begin to diminish. A realization of your own mortality begins to form within your mind and takes a secure seat within your consciousness. In other words, you come to a realization that everything you strive for here is only temporary. You look in the mirror one day and realize that the reflection you see staring back at you is one of a changing person. You see a body that is slowly diminishing, ultimately to pass way. If you are fortunate, you will come to a firm realization that the person staring back at you is really driven by the intelligence or soul residing within that temporary body, and not just by the physical nature itself. You slowly begin to come to a realization of a more eternal and permanent sense of self; a sense of self that strives to endure beyond the conclusion of the physical.

In other words, you begin to harbor a feeling, sense, hope or faith in an extension of self that somehow survives beyond life as it is known in mortality. This transition is mainly a spiritual and intuitive one, but it must occur for every individual if they are to begin to alleviate the fear of death and begin to fully realize the more divine potentials that reside within them. Priorities begin to shift. The material comforts and accumulation of worldly possessions becomes less important. More time and attention is given to important relationships, building reservoirs of knowledge and refining the sensitivities of spiritual things. Service to others becomes a valuable commodity as you begin to realize that a lifetime of your own experiences pays dividends through sharing time, abilities, resources and wisdom with others.

As you make this transitional transcendence to ideas of a more metaphysical nature you begin to realize that the only capital that has a chance of surviving this lifetime are the loving relationships you have developed and the truthful and lasting knowledge you accumulate. If in fact the nature of the spirit or soul is eternal, then nothing else is transferable. If you are effectively making a transcendent transition, you will increasingly focus on actions and potentials that feed into the capital of love and knowledge.

Epilogue: The Religious Metaphor of the Great Cliff

Envision the dynamics of this world as a great, towering cliff that extends from the ground up into the sky. The top of the cliff is not even visible from the ground, but disappears up into the clouds and the haze of lofty, almost unimaginable heights. The whole of humanity stands initially on the ground adjacent to this cliff. From the ground a series of natural rock stairways and pathways cascade vertically up the cliff. Some paths are short. Some are tremendously long and traverse large sections of the cliff. Many of the stairways come to ledges on the cliff. From the top of one stairway, the base of another stairway continues up the cliff from another point along a ledge. Some of the stairways climb the cliff to a point and end against a ledge with no further direction to go, risking a fall downward unless a retreat is made along the terminated path.

Beyond the top of the cliff lies a vast kingdom of unimaginable prosperity and joy. A place where there is no animosity, a place where love, wisdom and justice rule supreme. It is a land overflowing with abundance. The necessities of life are free and in never-ending supply. It is a place where age, illness and death are overcome and life continues in perfect health and balance. This land is ruled by a mighty King who rules with perfect peace, love and omniscience, and seeks only for the welfare and benefit of all who enter and make themselves worthy for this great land. All who enter this great kingdom, it is told, enjoy the peace and happiness associated with being freed from the worries and cares of life in the land below and along the cliff. All who dwell there find harmony and contentment one with another and are able to find true peace and the full meaning and potential of their souls. Every once in a while, reports come down of the majesty of the land beyond the top of the cliff. It is even reported that there a those privileged few who have travelled back down from the top of the cliff to encourage others to climb and seek the great abundances of the kingdom beyond the top of the cliff.

There are many at the base of the cliff who, upon learning the tales of such a beautiful and promised land, begin searching for and climbing the stairways they feel can bring them most safely to the top of the cliff. The stairways are steep, and once a seeker's climb has begun they must cling mightily to their respective stairway, lest they possibly fall and be dashed upon the ground below. Some climb a little ways and, discouraged by the rigors of the climb, descend back down and remain contentedly on the ground below. Others scoff at those climbing the stairway and berate them for wasting their time when the ground they are on already provides solid footing. Others climb up stairways that end at nothing upon the cliff and return to tell their story of frustration and failure, questioning the value of climbing the cliff at all. Yet others climb stairways that ascend far up the cliff, proceeding across ledges and up other stairways that bring them as high as they dare go. Many of these, once they have embarked upon such a journey, come to greatly enjoy the views and vistas that open to them as they climb higher up the cliff. They see the world below them from whence they came from a broader and fuller perspective. They become conditioned and accustomed to the rigors of the climb and lose fear of falling as they become committed to the journey.

Yet even these most dedicated climbers who diligently make the journey come to realize that none of the stairways actually make it to the very top of the cliff. The stairways all fall short to some extent or another. Some stairways make it very close to the top while others end with the top of the cliff still some distance away. But for those who undertake the journey and are determined at any cost to reach the top of the cliff, a marvelous miracle happens.

After they have they climbed as high as any stairway they can navigate will take them, and seem to be able to proceed no further up the cliff, a strong pair of hands lowers a rope to them and pulls them easily up and over the final precipice. They are greeted by perfect, loving beings who have reached out and helped them complete their journey to the paradise beyond the cliff. It is explained by these helpful "angels" that their assistance is always available for those who dare to chance the excursion up the cliff. Their journey from the land and life below complete, these travelers enter into the rest of the grand kingdom above, preparing for whatever marvels the next stage of their adventure might present.

In this metaphorical story, the ground below the cliff represents this world and the natural order that it follows. The cliff represents our spiritual journey through life and the ascension to our highest potentials and achievements. The stairways represent the philosophies, religions and moral and scientific codes to which we might subscribe. The ledges represent the values and rites that work to keep us focused on our code of beliefs, searching for higher and greater understanding. The land beyond the top of the cliff represents the idea of the continuation of life beyond the bounds of this world equivalent to the Judeo-Christian idea of heaven.

Chapter 7

<u>The Six Basic Assumptions Associated with Divine Human Potential</u>

As we have previously discussed, everything you do in life is based on certain sets of assumptions. For example, you assume you will rest, awaken the next day and move forward with whatever work or daily routine you are used to. You assume this because you have done it repeatedly time and time again. It works for others, it has worked for you. Our assumptions may certainly reflect our beliefs and models of the world, either as we have been taught or learned through direct experience. Not every assumption may be true or accurate. As you gain experience, you toss out assumptions that prove to be untrue or useless and replace them with different sets based on a progressing and maturing perspective.

Along with the assumptions in Chapter Two that help understand the nature of the Divine itself, the six assumptions below apply more individually and form a foundation for recognizing and unlocking your higher potentials, those that suggest intrinsic divinity. The key to understanding and applying any assumption is first to accept the possibilities the assumption suggests, then act according to those possibilities regularly in life routines, then finally look for and internalize the results that arise from wise application of the assumption. In essence, "the results speak for themselves."

Assumption 1 – <u>We are More than our Biological Parts and Processes</u>

The prevailing scientific frameworks seek to measure the finality of life in terms of biological parts and processes. It is as if the entire human experience is contained in the electrical activity of the human brain, supported by a musculoskeletal system given functionality by our cardiovascular system. Indeed it is productive to understand the wonders and the intricacies of the functions of the human body. The interesting leap that current science makes is to ascribe all activities and sum of being to these biological systems. In the typical logic of modern science, we can only accept what we can measure and study.

But many of the most formative human experiences are immeasurable. How can we dissect, weigh or make drawings of human experience such as love, devotion, emotional pain or disappointment? We can closely analyze, take a picture of and fix a broken foot. But how can we measure or fix a broken heart? And which event will have the more impactful or long-lasting effect on human potential? A foot or the feelings and actions ascribed to the heart?

We must operate under the simple assumption that the entirety of a human being is more than the measurable biological systems. We must assume another part, housed within our biology that contains the core essence of who we are. Call it karmic energy, the soul, the spirit of man; however you wish to categorize this scientifically unmeasured sense of self. If you can accept the fundamental premise of this assumption, you will begin to assess your daily feelings and decisions from a slightly different point of view. Over time, you will come to recognize this "spirit", this sense of inner self and will come to recognize that this part of you can react and exercise will to some degree independent of the biological demands of the body. In fact, like many sages, wise men and spiritual gurus from many different cultures, you may be able to apply control to a significant degree over your biology through this inner spiritual energy or power.

The point is that if you will operate under this assumption, you accelerate your ability to recognize and utilize this inner spirit in activating and exercising your higher potentials. And indeed, if you are able to recognize the broader and more enduring nature of such inner energy, your perspective will change to accommodate the potentials such a nature implies.

Assumption 2 – <u>Intelligence and Will are Capable of Expansion and Increase</u>

Human intelligence is a very broadly defined subject. While intelligence is often broken down into various categories for discussion and analysis such as spatial, mathematical, musical, interpersonal, naturalistic, kinesthetic and so forth, a more general definition would be helpful. For the sake of understanding and fulfilling your ultimate potentials intelligence is best defined as any process or ability to create both function and increase in your personal growth and understanding.

Intelligence is the force within you that allows you to comprehend your own ability to think, feel and act. Will is the direction or strength of your application of whatever intelligence you possess. These aspects of your existence are not fixed, but ever fluid and capable of change. With proper application intelligence can be increased throughout your life. With experience and wisdom, the will you apply to act upon your intelligence may also grow and increase in quality, reach and focus.

Just as these aspects may increase with applied diligence, with neglect they may also decrease. It is important to understand that these catalysts of potential are dynamic and always in flux. You can feed your intelligence with the acquisition of knowledge. Not just with internalization of fact, figures and trivia, but also with intuitive feelings, actions and observations of results.

The expansion of intelligence goes beyond just accumulating a catalog of more intricate cause and effect relationships gained through life experiences. It involves both understanding and feeling the larger implications of complex relationships and experiences as a contributing factor to potentials; to both your personal potentials and the potentials of those around you. The highest applications of increasing intelligence are to feed and nurture those potentials toward their highest expressions and fulfillment.

This implies that the application of intelligence towards the highest potentials will actually cycle and feed the increase of that intelligence through applied experience. While applications of intelligence toward self-centered, harmful or destructive means that limit or destroy potential will also eventually hinder the development of that intelligence.

Assumption 3 –You Must Apply the Process of Becoming; Law of the Harvest

As discussed in chapter 6, you must assume that you are always in the process of becoming. And a simple observation of human experience shows the efficacy of this assumption. We are indeed always in a process of development, either positive or negative. You are either becoming better at the things you value, or you are losing ground against time in regard to that knowledge, skill or potential. There is little neutral ground. You are either increasing your understanding or increasing your ignorance of all the available possibilities that surround you. This is an inescapable human dynamic. You must embrace this dynamic to your benefit or ignore it to your detriment.

To many, the idea of a constant state of becoming might seem arduous or intimidating. But when looked at through the lens of achieving potentials, the idea of becoming should seem more natural. In a sense, becoming should be viewed as the natural flow of a river. Water cascades downstream seemingly without effort, even though there are many obstacles to a smooth flow. The force of the process of moving water either moves around obstacles or eventually overcomes them, sweeping them away. So it is with each of us. The dynamic of becoming will naturally carry you forward. The biggest difference is that you must choose the direction that your potential will flow in the current of becoming. This requires the exercise of will, and that exercise of will requires a fundamental understanding that your ultimate potentials must be tied to this process of becoming.

You must ultimately develop judgment and wisdom to assess which obstacles to your becoming need to be moved around and which need to be swept away. The only difference between the two is degree of effort and attention. This ultimately comes down to your own decision on which potentials hold the most value to you. You are the one in charge of determining which potentials get the most attention, both in terms of development and the overcoming of any barriers to that potential.

The concept of positive and negative potentials needs to be recognized when trying to embrace this becoming. You must clearly understand the law of the harvest: "As you sow so shall you reap." This is most forceful when applied in the context of becoming. Your efforts, your focus, your time and how you utilize and develop every skill and ability will eventually have a payoff. The potentials that are recognized, activated and developed within you will do so in direct correlation to the effort and attention you give them. There are no shortcuts, there are no free alternatives. Time and experience are the only crucibles in which your potentials can be appropriately mixed.

Assumption 4 – <u>You are Constantly Required to Exercise Will</u>

Along with the inherent dynamic of becoming is the idea that you are the one responsible for exercising your own free will under any circumstances. This applies in the most relaxed of situations or the most dire. There is not a waking moment in your day where you are not completely responsible for the decisions that you make. You cannot assign blame or responsibility to anyone else. You may react to the circumstances pressures or even coercions around you, but in the end it is always your call.

Viktor Frankl's groundbreaking work on cognitive psychology as outlined in his book "On Freedom and Dignity" emphasizes this idea of ultimate freedom of will. In his account, being incarcerated in a German concentration camp, he ultimately came to a revelatory discovery. He could curse his enemy and die, as many of his fellow campmates did, or he could choose to overcome the hatred and destruction that such a situation brought and love and serve anyone and everyone around him, even his enemies, for as long as he was able. It was this realization of complete freedom of choice in the worst of circumstances that gave him the strength and courage to survive while most around him experiencing the same deprivations deteriorated and died.

This internalization of complete responsibility of choice is the key to growth of any and every potential. You must choose to become and exercise will to participate in the activities that increase those potentials. Again, no one can do it for you. Yet, investment in your own potentials guarantees a direct return on your investment. If you exercise your free will to explore and develop your potentials, you achieve a direct return on that effort via personal growth and understanding. That others around you may benefit from the development of your potentials is an important but corollary result. You cannot control the will, and thus the receptive or contrary decisions of others, only your own.

Assumption 5 – <u>You Can Always Change the Direction and Slope of Potentials</u>

It follows naturally that if you accept the premise that you are always becoming and that you must constantly exercise your will to direct that process of becoming, you also have the capacity to change the direction and possible outcomes of the development of any and all potentials. If you do not like the way things are going and are unsatisfied with the results, change something! It is your decision, first and last. You may not have control over all of the variables surrounding you, but you still have capacity to change what you can change, even down to your own perceptions and attitudes.

Sometimes some of the greatest successes in life begin as a very small change in attitude or perception. Even a small change in course can, over time, result in large results from a small change. This can be either positive or negative depending upon your choices. To choose to pursue your potentials and seek positive slope or growth from those potentials should be followed by numerous small, daily choices to follow attitudes and actions that will reinforce your ideas of positive growth.

Every minute of every day you must make choices. Even when choosing to do nothing you have made a choice. The cumulative direction and slope of these individual choices defines the slope of your

pg. 166

potentials. Every minute of every day you have the capacity to accelerate the positive. You also have the ability to check a negative slope once you are aware of it.

Change is not necessarily a linear process. It is easy to regress into old habits, old ways of thinking. The point is to always look upward in terms of your potentials. Seek to lift yourself. Seek to lift others. If you fall, get back up. Extend a hand to others and open their eyes to their potentials and you will find you come to understand your own more thoroughly. If you approach your life with such an attitude you will discover that over time, months and years ahead, you accumulate wisdom through experience.

The mathematics of continuing to trend upward, always seeking positive change and positive slope to your potentials, adds up to a tremendous sum of understanding and personal knowledge over time. You begin to more clearly see the "human condition" as described by your own experience and not through the experience or philosophies of others. Your progress and potentials become uniquely yours, even though they are commonly shared by many others. It is their responsibility to frame their potentials in their own way, constantly seeking the same upward changes, though in their own way and experience. The power of the commonality of positive change cannot be understated, especially as it applies to building positive relationships with each other.

Effecting change presumes that you have built an understanding adequate enough to assess and evaluate the situation of negative slope and negative results. The principles taught in this book should be a mere starting point for understanding the dynamics of change. Only time and experience can instill depth and greater efficacy to the potentials you ultimately recognize and choose to develop. This process of development will be discussed in greater detail in the next chapter.

Assumption 6 – <u>Your Existence is Best Seen as a Chapter in A Larger Work.</u>

As you analyze your own potentials and possibilities, you must discover the perspective that comes from assuming that every action in your life has purpose and is not lost or in vain. If you operate under the assumption that your life is a small but important scene in a much larger, grander play, then you will innately assume responsibility to act your part well.

If you can come to internalize and embrace the seven assumptions associated with divine potential, you also must embrace the assumption that there is both continuation and purpose to your life and actions. Such purpose can be expressed as a record and measurement of your actions based on the very potentials you have identified and nurtured. If there is to be any presumed purpose to an individual life, the most simple and fundamental assumption to that purpose is growth and improvement. And the second most basic assumption is that such growth and purpose will eventually be framed in a larger and more extensive set of purposes. No life has to be lived in vain.

Our current comprehension of or inexperience with the greater possibilities that may supersede our lives here is not of primary importance. What is important is that we either operate on an assumption that our actions will eventually fit in to a grander scheme, along with some semblance of accountability in whatever role we might play in such a scheme, versus an assumption that life that is random and meaningless, and ultimately involves no accountability.

It is a simple conclusion to see that an assumption of accountability in a larger work, one greater than the sum of an individual life, effects discipline and responsibility of self, especially when it comes to activating your highest potentials. To assume that life is random and has no purpose beyond what you see, feel and experience while alive on earth creates a sense of purposelessness and ultimate doom. It breeds a fear of the end of mortal life and leaves little room for an ongoing accounting of accomplishment and memory that exceeds only those lives we have touched.

When acting out of fear or out of a limited perspective, it is easy to ignore the dynamics of higher potentials. Life revolves around the needs of the moment and little else. If there is no internal concept of greater purpose, there is a lack of perspective and motivation for responsibility to anything greater than the requirements of the day. A sense of nobility of self is lost in such a lack of perspective.

To truly see yourself as part of a greater work, a perception that will eventually resonate with the highest potentials you may achieve, both within the confines of the life you live and far beyond, offers an opening of perspective that has few limits when it comes to seeking and realizing your greatest potentials. Call the concept "eternal memory". Think of it as a realization that every action, thought and ambition can be recorded within your own memory and experience, as well as on the ledgers of a greater book. A book that embraces the cumulative actions of all of humanity without bias and with only the hope of realizing the highest and most enduring potentials for each of us; a universal ledger of everlasting accomplishment and potential.

Epilogue: A Universal Database?

The body of near death literature has burgeoned in the last decade or so. Out-of-body near death experiences were considered taboo just a few short decades ago, often rejected by behavioral professionals as illegitimate, delusional or fostered by some abnormal biological or brain activity in asphyxiated individuals. In the mid-twentieth century, just sharing such an experience could bring serious societal consequences and result in a very detrimental labelling of the recipient of such an experience. But the fact is, such experiences have been occurring as long as humans have been around. The seminal work that broke open a study of the genre was published by Dr. George F Richie , describing his 1943 near death experience in his ground breaking book "Return from Tomorrow" (1978, Baker House Book Co.). Dr. Ritchie's book inspired Raymond Moody's series entitled "Life after Life", and the rest is history.

While the discussion of the legitimacy of such experiences is a subject worthy of its own debate, a study of the literature reveals numerous commonalities that individuals experience that are independent of their religion, culture or upbringing. One of these experiences is known as the "life review". In Dr. Ritchie's experience this phenomenon is most remarkably recounted. After having been separated from his body and confronted by a Divine Being, Dr. Ritchie recounts the following:

"For into that room, along with His radiant presence- simultaneously, though in telling about it I have to describe them one by one- had also entered every single episode of my entire life. Everything that had ever happened to me was simply there, in full view, contemporary and current, all seemingly taking place at that moment.

There were episodes from my high school years – dates, chemistry exams, running the fastest mile in our school. I saw my graduation, saw myself entering the University of Richmond. And all the while I watched myself hold my stiff-necked aloofness from my mother, from my brother Henry, even little Bruce Gordon. I saw Dad coming home in his Major's uniform, saw myself going down to the post office to enlist for active service. I watched the mustering-in process at Camp Lee, watched myself and hundreds of other recruits boarding the train for Camp Barkely...

Every detail of twenty years of living was there to be looked at, the good, the bad, the high points, the-run-of-the-mill. And with this all-inclusive view came a question. It was implicit in every scene and, like the scenes themselves, seemed to proceed from the living Light beside me.

What did you do with your life?

It was obviously not a question in the sense that He was seeking information, for what I had done with my life was in plain view. In any case this total recalling, detailed and perfect, came from Him, not me. I could not have remembered a tenth of what was there until He showed it to me.

pg. 170

It seemed to be a question about values, not facts…hadn't I done anything lasting, anything important? I looked around me for something that would seem worthwhile in the light of this blazing Reality."

"Return From Tomorrow", pgs. 50-52.

Accepting Dr. Ritchie's account on its face, apart from the obvious implications this singular event has in terms of developing potentials, there is another fascinating aspect to the experience. Where did all of the detailed information of his life come from in this review? Does this imply that there exists a sort of "Universal Database"? A place within the cosmos where every action, every detail and every thought of all existence is recorded down to the minutest detail? The information had to come from somewhere. But where precisely? Even if it is postulated that it came from some subconscious recess of Dr. Ritchie's dying brain, it was still recorded somewhere to be summoned in a highly organized fashion at the time of this event.

The implications of Dr. Ritchie's testimony are profound and far reaching. It speaks directly to the principle of personal accountability, and suggests that each moment we spend in matters both trivial and important, may be subject to a specific accountability at some point in the future. It also suggest that every moment of every life, your life, my life, all of our lives, must somehow be precious and important for every detail of such information to be recorded within the fabric of the universe. Serious food for thought when considering the divine nature of our existence.

Chapter 8

The Six Levels of Comprehending and Internalizing Your Potential

While you must initially exercise a belief in your own innate potentials, over time obedience to the idea and principle that your potentials do exist and can grow in a positive slope and direction yield a harvest of comprehension and internalization. But you do not become complete in the exercise of your potentials overnight. It is literally a lifelong, ongoing process. There will always be barriers to personal internalization of potential. Barriers of circumstance, barriers of perception and barriers of self-doubt.

Barriers of circumstance occur when you are exercising correct behavior in terms of a given potential, but the current environment or circumstance interferes with your behaviors. A simple example would be to wish to run a timed mile on a day when the temperature has dropped below zero and a blinding snowstorm has moved in. You wish to put in the mileage, but a good fire might be a better idea on such a day. Circumstance can deny you resources to activate and internalize potential. Sometimes, you have to do what circumstance allows. You are not responsible beyond that.

Barriers of perception are more difficult. Every individual has "blind spots". These are areas of perception and behavior that simply have not registered in our conscious perception. Until we "see" the value of our potential, we cannot activate that potential. We are not responsible until that potential is perceived as "within reach". Awareness of your potentials is just a beginning. To understand is not the same as being determined to "go and do". You need that motivation even after barriers of perception are lowered.

Self-doubt is perhaps the most difficult barrier. The modern world seems to be moving further down the instant gratification spectrum. Personal potentials is a long term undertaking. It would not take much to become discouraged as results from seeking potential does not show immediate progress or reward. Long term effort, often years, even decades, in scope, is a necessity when focusing on personal growth and progress. When immediate rewards are not obvious, doubt is the first remedy for such a situation. It is easy to give up or move on before tangible results are ever realized.

However, your potentials, once recognized and focused upon, may progress through any of these six levels of comprehension. Each individual potential may progress as you exercise it independently. Some potentials may progress together. It depends upon the innate attention you give to each aspect of what is good, right and divine within you. It depends on your consistency and diligence as to how you progress through the various levels of internalization.

It is unusual for a degree of understanding to come quickly. Even if your experiences should be permeated with numerous "aha" moments, the cumulative effect of your potentials is gradual. Day after day, month after month, year by year you must remain consistent. Growth in any potential requires both experience and time. Time to live through various experiences and time to ponder and internalize the lessons and growth from those experiences.

The six levels of comprehending and internalizing your potential offers a framework of evaluation that can be applied as you reflect on where a specific potential is on a scale of personal application and internalization. Please note that no specific sense of measurement other than these levels is offered in the Salvation Equation. Unlike a finite measure such as feet or yards, the measurement of potentials varies as much as each individual. We are all uniquely programmed and progress along our own timelines. Again, from the perspective of the Salvation Equation, progress should at least be considered in a positive slope, a slope in proximity to the opportunities and potentials you may discover and develop.

Your progress is a very personal endeavor. While it is difficult to measure many aspects of the development of potential, some aspects are measureable. You can see progress, for example, in your personal fitness levels as you undertake regular exercise. You can see professional growth as you master certain technical aspects of a job. You can see deeper and more meaningful relationships among those close to you as you focus on important principles and actions your potentials might suggest. Each potential is generally subjective, unless that particular potential has an actual physical measurement that can serve as a guide. In that sense, potentials and the level of internalization serve as a helpful barometer to "know thyself". Below, we outline the six levels of comprehending and internalizing your potential:

Level 1 - Blind acceptance from another source.

At the most base level, you accept that you have a potential because someone or something informs you that you do. We can become cognizant, to a very low degree, because we are given outside messages that persuade us that there is truth to the idea. The traditional picture of a father and son learning to throw and catch a baseball in the back yard comes to mind. "Son, you are a natural athlete" the father chimes as his boy catches at least half of the balls lobbed his way. The boy, on a conscious or sub-conscious level, registers that message and finds joy in running, jumping, throwing, catching, etc. In essence, he is blindly obedient to the idea of potential, even if it is not richly experienced at this level.

Level 2 - Forming behaviors and attitudes to avoid punishment.

At this level, you learn to use skill and actions that are described by a specific potential to avoid any negative consequences. In the baseball analogy, the message might be given at a little league game: "Son, you had better catch the ball when it is hit to you, or you will be pulled from the game." The desire to play is enforced by exercise of physical concentration on the ball game. The motivation is not the potential itself, but a fear of consequence of the actions the potential describes are not consistently performed.

Level 3 - Forming behaviors and attitudes to obtain a reward.

At this level, you begin to recognize that exercising your potentials may bring desired rewards. Whether these rewards are physical, emotional/intellectual or both is not important. Here you gain recognition of ability to learn, grow and perform for some reward that achievement may bring. Continuing the baseball analogy, the teams coach may say "Ice cream for everyone that gets a hit in today's game". The vision of that reward may inspire focus in the boy who can clearly associate his athletic ability to hit a ball with his love of ice cream.

Level 4 - Seeing potential as a beneficial choice.

At this level, you move away from the criteria of an external punishment or reward to a more internal value that you begin to associate with a given potential. The value of a given potential will certainly be framed and colored by the society in which you live, but the positive slope of any potential will share certain universal associations that can be considered "beneficial". If you or others around you are enriched by the actions that flow from a potential, you are bound to make a positive association. In our baseball analogy, let us assume that our player is several years older. He may recognize that to hone his athletic potential contributes to the overall play of his team, and they have a goal to win the city championship in their division. Thus his choice to develop the abilities surrounding his potential may contribute to more than his own achievement and satisfaction.

Level 5 - Seeing potential as the highest virtue.

At this level, you begin to see the potential you have developed as the best possible pathway to being the very best that you can be in a given endeavor. You associate that potential with the highest possible virtues. You strive to be the best; you enjoy focusing on the best actions you may exercise. You have highly internalized the values, principles and actions associated with a given potential. In a world of many possible outcomes, you view the application of a potential as the absolute best possible outcome. Time and experience have provided significant reinforcement to confirm that the potential you have developed and applied over time is indeed beneficial and meets all of the tests of a positive potential.

In our ball player analogy, we see a grown man now playing professional ball. Not only have the skills he has learned over many years of applying athletic principles to his game provided him with a notable career, he is engaged with his community and provides inspiration for other players hoping to achieve a similar professional status. He works constantly at improving his game and seeks excellence on and off the field. As a result, he will touch the lives of many others over his career, as well as create unparalleled memories for himself.

Level 6 - Internalizing and becoming your potential.

At this level, the lines between you and the potential within dissolve. The highest applications of that potential become literally who you are. Through time, experience, thoughtful reflection, continuous application you become a walking embodiment of the principles a potential engenders. You behave consistently and without interruption according to the highest values within that potential. You have had so much experience and can point to numerous instances of success so that you would simply choose to be nothing less.

In our ballplayer analogy, we equate this level of internalization to a hall-of-fame career. Years of application, achievement, success and recognition lead to an individual who experiences athleticism at its highest level. Their name defines the game, such as Hank Aaron, Connie Mack or Nolan Ryan. They in essence become an integral part of the game and its history.

It is the ultimate goal of the Salvation Equation to encourage you to internalize every possible potential to the highest levels. Keep in mind that this is a process. And a process that can extend across a lifetime and beyond. If mankind was meant to experience and achieve, what greater purpose could there be than to strive to internalize and become every positive potential that we may have an opportunity to experience? It is a question for the ages, and one where the answer should be glaringly obvious.

Epilogue: An Inconvenient Continuum

It should be apparent that the Salvation Equation is primarily about pushing your boundaries, questioning your assumptions and reaching for the highest potentials you possesses, and reaching a point where each and every potential you may resonate with throughout your life becomes internalized. In short, your greatest aspects of self, driving an increasing and sharpened view of self-worth, become who you are, affecting everything you do in your daily life. While the best and highest use of those potentials is in the service of self and others, what about the consequences of such personal progress in the larger spectrum of "normal society".

A current term used to describe individuals and achievements beyond the normal is the word "outlier". By definition, to develop your highest potentials includes the risk that you will begin to outpace or overachieve compared to the societal norm. You will indeed begin to stand out, even if those achievements are humble in comparison. History teaches us that outliers in a "normal" society do indeed take on a certain amount of risk.

Some outliers are celebrated, such as Ghandi, Mother Theresa or Confucius. The extraordinary positive achievement in their chosen life pursuits, utilizing their potentials and talents to a high degree, earn such individuals places of honor in the idealistic retrospective of history. But such lives and such achievements are never without controversy. It is often the greatest criticism of outliers that somehow they upset the order that "normal" society wished to preserve. Personal change, as well as societal change, is almost always accompanied by discomfort and social cost.

Other outliers throughout history may be rightly vilified, such as Hitler, Ivan the Terrible or Caligula. Individuals who take enormous potentials to the negative end of the scale often bring havoc not only to their own lives, but to the lives of numerous other victims. When tremendous potential is turned to the negative entire societies may be forced to suffer under the leadership or decisions of the perpetrators of poorly used potentials through power.

In either case, the achieving outlier runs the risk of being viewed "outside the norm". Again, this can be a positive as an inspiration, or negative as a vilification. A simple continuum would look something like this:

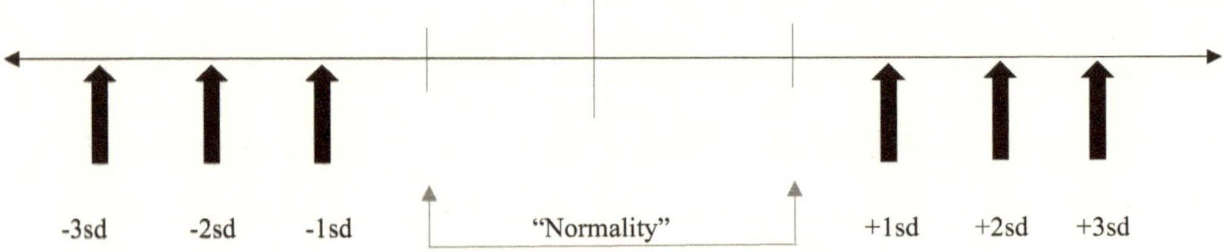

As you progress one, two or three standard deviations from "normal", you will tend to stand out as an achiever, a living example of one aspiring to reach towards your highest potentials. This is not without consequence. Those consequences will be a direct result of the slope of your potentials. The more positive, the more the likelihood of a reaction of admiration. The more negative, the more likely you are building a life of infamy.

But positive aspirations do not always bring positive consequences. These positive desires and actions based on potential can bring difficult consequences when "normality, or the existing socio-political system is set to punish such potentials. Joan of Arc and the reverend John Rogers suffered similar fates. Both were burned at the stake. Joan of Arc for leading the French to an inspired victory over British occupiers at Orleans in The Hundred Year War, and Reverend Rogers for instituting Protestant reformation in a predominantly Catholic Europe and daring, among other things, to suggest that full English translations of the Bible be provided to the masses.

When the system has moved away from a healthy normality, achieving positive potentials may have unintended difficult consequences. Such is the nature of an inconvenient continuum. The principles of the Salvation Equation, if exercised widely, would create a "normal" that encouraged individual potential and progress in light of the assumptions that it entails. In such a social system, positive standard deviations would almost always engender reward, not derision or abhorrence of peculiarity. These are foundations of true peace in the world, and cooperation within societies.

Chapter 9

The Foremost Key Core Potential: Capacity for Love; the Nature and Scope of Love

As mentioned earlier, the idea of love as it relates to our highest potentials is core to the entire premise of the Salvation Equation. The capacity for love is the highest and most preeminent potential of all. The nature and scope of the love referred to here requires additional clarifying. If there has ever been a subject more written about, more dramatized and more romanticized over the centuries, love must be the most widely publicized. If the question were ever to be asked, "what is the central philosophy of heaven", the answer could only be "Love". The assumptions we make about the divine and the nature of God break down without the constant and universal guiding principle of love.

But what is meant exactly by this definition of love? After all, so much has been written about love that it qualifies as the most informed subject of the ages. There is always the ever present romantic love. There is love within families, brotherly love, love of learning, love of science, love of art, love of nature and so on. Love can be utilized on so many levels. But in the purest and most applicable sense, is there an overarching definition of love that can encompass and clarify any other type or application of love?

The Salvation Equation suggests that there is, and that the purest definition of love resides in the fact that each one of us has fabulous and important potentials waiting to be discovered at some point in our journey. In this context the most helpful and enabling definition of love would be as follows:

"Love is the conscious (or subconscious) choice to put the positive becoming of another equal to or greater than the positive becoming of oneself"

The first part of this definition of love suggests that love is a choice. In popular literature, the focus is so often on the effects of love and the romanticized actions that are driven by love that the actual basis for love is overlooked. Love is more than the dreamy associations you may experience in a romantic relationship. Those are symptoms of the underlying issue. The escalated heartbeat, increased body temperature and hormone levels are not a driving force, but indicators of a deeper process.

Nevertheless, love ultimately *is* a choice. In that choice you determine that the becoming, or the potential of another, is at least equal to your own. In that choice you are choosing a number of related actions. Those actions include nurturing, encouraging, serving, supporting, helping, teaching, listening, learning and so many other behaviors that will allow another to grow. When this idea of love is applied to an idea versus other individuals, it is manifest in a desire for the highest and best application and understanding of that idea.

Not all decisions of love bring emotional euphoria. Sometimes love is simply work, complete with dedication and sacrifice. But love will always be intrinsically satisfying to the one exercising it. It will always lift, refine, and contribute greatly to each and every potential you may pursue, as well as provide enhancement of the potentials of others. Love is the great key. It is the key to all sustainable relationships and positive interpersonal dynamics.

But love is even more than that. Love is positive and moving force. Such love builds families, it builds homes and communities. Such love can inspire nations built on the freedoms and principles that would allow love to reign free among every citizen. Love is at the heart of innovation and invention. Love is behind all positive intelligence. Indeed, if we are to accept the Divine, and anything that is lasting and eternal, love must be the primary force behind all that the term eternal might suggest. Indeed, if the motivations behind God or any higher intelligence were ever to be understood, it must be understood through this sort of love. Love is indeed that very power by which all creation has come into existence. For all creation of necessity must progress according to principles of love.

For love is the one force, power or quantity that can never encourage the negative, harmful or temporary. Love reaches into the loftiest areas of our life, our world our universe and always encourages to continue upward. Love is always positive and always gives hope. Love encourages every positive thought and action you could ever hope to undertake. Love is the potential behind all others that lift and sustain. Love always prompts you to become, and to become more, greater and brighter in everything positive. When you truly love, you reach beyond yourself and have a sincere desire for anyone and everyone else to become in similar positive ways.

Further, if you are to assume that God exists, and work on any basis of such assumptions, you must also assume that love as herein defined is the central and operative force that defines both your potential and the entire concept of God. If love by definition encompasses all positive becoming, then everything that exists and has become or will become whatever it was designed or created to be will be subject to love. In short, your life, the planet you live on and the universe in which you find yourself has been and will continue to be subject to such love. So broad and pervasive is this force, this idea, this energy of love that if it did not exist then neither would we. Neither would our world exist nor would it have any place among all creation. Love predates and presupposes everything we know, love was there first. And it is love that keeps it all moving forward and continuing to become and progress. And that includes you and me.

And it is that process of becoming that is central to an accurate definition of love. Without becoming, without a benefit in the transaction of any relationship, that relationship has no power to lift, improve, sustain or empower yourself or another. It ultimately takes up time at best, or becomes harmful and degrading at its worst. Positive becoming, the natural support of increasing potential, can always define caring at its highest level in a relationship. And that is the key to love. Love will always lift and inspire. Love seeks always to improve. Love adheres to potential and drives it upward, forward and onward in every possible positive way.

And you should never overlook the inherent implication of the definition that such love also involves you. To place the positive becoming of another equal to or greater than your own presupposes you are committed to your own potential and understand how it works within you. The blind cannot lead the blind. To see the great potential in others, to love them and be devoted to that potential and the becoming it implies, you must work from your own base of understanding. You must place value on your positive becoming, understanding the fruits it will bear, and having the faith and courage to enable another. In other words, you must apply such power of love to yourself in order to fully apply it to anyone else.

And love is indeed a courageous decision. Hate, envy, strife, jealousy and all other negative associations are easy in comparison. To love requires dedication, courage and work. It may come naturally and easily at times, but it is always a result of focus and dedication, of sacrifice and sensitivity. Love will always require you to commit and work for another, but it will return to you dividends in terms of your own potential.

One of the most important, and perhaps most obvious, applications of this concept of love is in the area of relationships, particularly in relationships where oversight, power or authority is involved. Whether it is a relationship between two or more individuals, a family, a town or a great nation, this definition of love applies universally in matters of interpersonal relationship, management and governance.

Intrinsic in this definition of love is the idea that only through an accurate vision of love can a lasting foundation of understanding, cooperation and mutual benefit exist. While any law, oath, obligation, commitment or contract can be originated through numerous other criteria, when it comes to the relationships of individuals only this foundation of love can establish a sustainable, lasting and continually beneficial relationship. On a foundation of anything less, that relationship will eventually change, expire, crumble or otherwise fade away.

In a one on one personal relationship, a focus on the positive potential of another is a powerful bond that strengthens any relationship. The very act of seeking the best for another lifts anyone who honestly strives for it. If everyone within your sphere of influence operated clearly by this definition of love, you would not only trust each one of these associates, but would clearly have some degree of focus on their needs as well. Only in a commitment of love that seeks the best in another can a sustained and nurturing relationship exist.

The implication for the management, leadership or governance of large groups is even more profound. This definition of love suggests that policies that do not consider this application of love as it relates to the potential of others will have lesser efficacy by the simple fact they do not address the core issue that can successfully sustain group dynamics. That simple core issue is the love needed to bring out the greater good of the group by allowing each individual potential to thrive under the protection of that love. While group dynamics can be managed short term through lesser demanding, tempting, oppressive or even deadly criteria, these systems inevitably will break down over time under their own lack of love, or lack of allowing potential to develop and become. History contains a consistent record of individuals and peoples seeking to flee or shake off any system of governance that does not take love and the freedoms of becoming that our potentials suggest into consideration.

Also encompassed in this definition of love is the corollary of what love is not. Love is, in most cases, not a self-serving process. It is selfless. When another individual is objectified, viewed as less than oneself, or seen as simply a means to an end, love is not fully involved in the relationship. This is particularly applicable in relationships between partners, where personal desires and lusts may be substituted for the idea of love. That physical or emotional relationships continue between consenting individuals is not at issue. What is most important is the central focus of that relationship. Is that focus self-serving or selfless?

Is it only the satisfaction one party receives out of the relationship, no matter the cost or consideration of the other? Is it a mutual benefit that involves a satisfaction without consideration of the growth or potential of the other? Is it exploitative or abusive in any manner? All of these dynamics in a relationship fall short of the fundamental criteria of love as defined in this chapter. In other words, we should not view love exclusively in terms of what another person can give you, but in terms of the benefits and growth towards positive potential you can engender in one another.

This also suggests the need for a healthy and coherent understanding of love. It may be argued that many of the most significant social ills facing society today center around the breakdown in relationships between the sexes. Where a more selfless and subservient definition of love has cemented couples and families together in the past, along with the work, sacrifice and mutual considerations that accompany a focus on the becoming and sustaining of each other, the more modern and "hip" perspectives have moved the focus to self-centered paradigms of love. Paradigms that become inevitably unsustainable. In essence, without an understanding of the central, selfless dynamic of love, namely the positive becoming of another, the relationship inevitably weakens or breaks down altogether when built on lesser criteria.

If history has proven any simple social truth, it is that the family is the cornerstone of society. Where strong family relationships exist, strong communities exist. Where strong communities exist, a nation as a whole is generally socially healthy. The definition of love as given here is the fundamental core of building and maintaining a healthy relationship between a committed partners, mother and father and between parents and children. It is critical to the maintenance of healthy, functional and nurturing families. Just the sort of families that can ensure generational continuance and functional society. Without this level of love applied within the walls of a home, the society itself is at risk.

One of the great social problems affecting family and strong functional societal relationships is the lessening or removal of these higher ideals of love from relationships within the family. Lesser substitutes are introduced over time through modified cultural norms that have less power to encourage, lift and guide members within the immediate and extended family groups toward their higher potentials. One particular aspect that has become noticeably prevalent over the last century or more is the substitution of contractual relationship versus covenant relationships.

The Contractual versus Covenant application of Love

The definition of love as required by the Salvation Equation can best be summed up in the comparison of a contract versus covenant relationship. The best way to describe the erosion of love between individuals today is to suggest that modern relationships have moved continually away from a covenant relationship and are now firmly entrenched in the idea of a contract relationship. The Salvation Equation posits that a contract relationship is by nature an inferior basis for a relationship between individuals. While a society may function for a time on a contract basis, the foundation of contract relationships is fundamentally infirm, as the basis for that relationship can change quickly with time or circumstance.

The basis for contract relationship lies in "the art of the deal". Contract relationships are built on the expectations of outcomes for each party. Every person in a contract relationship is focused on "what is in it for me". In a marriage or family situation, the basis for contract relationships often revolve around looks, sex, status, social position or financial capabilities. Many marriages or other cooperative relationships are often based primarily around the lifestyle that such a union is expected to provide. And these are not necessarily unimportant criteria. The issue is, they should not be the preeminent or overriding criteria. The most accurate application of love states that the becoming of each individual in the relationship should take priority over other criteria.

In a contract relationship, the relationship can erode, breakdown and ultimately end if certain expectations in the contract relationship are taken away over time. Looks may fade with age; a bad economy may decimate earning power; illness or other unforeseen considerations enter unexpectedly into lives creating trials that require great patience in suffering. Any number of circumstances not anticipated in the original contract may, and often do, occur. In a strictly contract relationship, one or both parties may decide the contract (that is the initial and ongoing expectations of "the deal") have been violated. Unfortunately, in many instances such circumstances trigger the inevitable end of the contract, and the relationship falls apart.

This is not to understate that there are instances in any relationship that may create irresolvable differences. Abuse, deception, infidelity, extreme illness or incapacity can greatly impact the previous dynamics of a relationship. And there are justifiable solutions to any such difficulties. Again, the issue is the central focus, the basis for expectations within that relationship. If the relationship terminates based on criteria outside the becoming of the individuals, it may be based on temporary benefits that can wilt under the changes of time or circumstance.

A covenant relationship differs from a contract relationship in one critically important aspect. The covenant relationship revolves around a two way promise between individuals to put the positive becoming of the other individual at the forefront of the relationship. The primary focus of a covenant relationship is not "what is in it for me", but "who can we become together" within the parameters of the relationship. This implies that whatever other social criteria are built into the relationship, the overriding focus will be on the mutual growth and ultimate potentials of the individuals in the relationship.

Such a central focus has much more power to endure changing circumstances. The needs of the each other will supersede needs for lifestyle, finance or lesser social contracts. The emphasis is that happiness, as expressed through growth and becoming, is centered in each other, and not just the circumstances through which the relationship travels over time. It reinforces the powerful bond that can be built within family, and establishes family and functioning households as a bulwark against the blowing winds of societal change or upheaval. It reinforces that no matter what external circumstance might occur, the positive becoming of each individual takes precedent over all.

Covenant relationships create an environment where love can find broader application. It defines the dynamics between individuals as love centered versus outcome centered. In almost any imaginable instance, a covenant relationship will inevitably bring long term satisfaction in greater degree than a contract relationship. A covenant relationship, by nature, will stand more firmly against the tests time and changes life may throw at it. Where such love is active between individuals, looking forward to shared becoming, a firmer foundation for family and society in general is built.

Epilogue: Mother Theresa

It is difficult to find a more outstanding modern example of the application of love in action, as defined in this chapter, as well as an illustration of the potential for service, than the life and works of Mother Theresa. Mother Teresa was born on August 26, 1910, in Skopje, the current capital of the Republic of Macedonia as Agnes Gonxha Bojaxhiu. In 1919, when Mother Teresa — then Agnes — was only eight years old, her father suddenly fell ill and died. While the cause of his death remains unknown, many have speculated that political enemies poisoned him.

In the aftermath of her father's death, Agnes became extraordinarily close to her mother, a pious and compassionate woman who instilled in her daughter a deep commitment to charity. Although by no means wealthy, Drana Bojaxhiu extended an open invitation to the city's destitute to dine with her family. "My child, never eat a single mouthful unless you are sharing it with others," she counseled her daughter. When Agnes asked who the people eating with them were, her mother uniformly responded, "Some of them are our relations, but all of them are our people." In 1928, an 18-year-old Agnes Bojaxhiu decided to become a nun and set off for Ireland to join the Sisters of Loreto in Dublin. It was there that she took the name Sister Mary Teresa after Saint Thérèse of Lisieux.

A year later, Sister Mary Teresa traveled on to Darjeeling, India, for the novitiate period.
Afterward she was sent to Calcutta, where she was assigned to teach at Saint Mary's High School
for Girls, a school run by the Loreto Sisters and dedicated to teaching girls from the city's
poorest Bengali families. Sister Teresa learned to speak both Bengali and Hindi fluently as she
taught geography and history and dedicated herself to alleviating the girls' poverty through
education.

On September 10, 1946, Mother Teresa experienced a second calling, the "call within a call" that
would forever transform her life. She was riding in a train from Calcutta to the Himalayan
foothills for a retreat when she said Christ spoke to her and told her to abandon teaching to work
in the slums of Calcutta aiding the city's poorest and sickest people.

Mother Teresa quickly translated her calling into concrete actions to help the city's poor. She
began an open-air school and established a home for the dying destitute in a dilapidated building
she convinced the city government to donate to her cause. In October 1950, she won canonical
recognition for a new congregation, the Missionaries of Charity, which she founded with only a
handful of members—most of them former teachers or pupils from St. Mary's School.

As the ranks of her congregation swelled and donations poured in from around India and across
the globe, the scope of Mother Teresa's charitable activities expanded exponentially. Over the
course of the 1950s and 1960s, she established a leper colony, an orphanage, a nursing home, a
family clinic and a string of mobile health clinics.

In 1971, Mother Teresa traveled to New York City to open her first American-based house of charity, and in the summer of 1982, she secretly went to Beirut, Lebanon, where she crossed between Christian East Beirut and Muslim West Beirut to aid children of both faiths. In 1985, Mother Teresa returned to New York and spoke at the 40th anniversary of the United Nations General Assembly. While there, she also opened Gift of Love, a home to care for those infected with HIV/AIDS.

In February 1965, Pope Paul VI bestowed the Decree of Praise upon the Missionaries of Charity, which prompted Mother Teresa to begin expanding internationally. By the time of her death in 1997, the Missionaries of Charity numbered more than 4,000 — in addition to thousands more lay volunteers — with 610 foundations in 123 countries around the world.

The Decree of Praise was just the beginning, as Mother Teresa received various honors for her tireless and effective charity. She was awarded the Jewel of India, the highest honor bestowed on Indian civilians, as well as the now-defunct Soviet Union's Gold Medal of the Soviet Peace Committee. In 1979, Mother Teresa was awarded the Nobel Peace Prize in recognition of her work "in bringing help to suffering humanity. By 1996, Teresa operated 517 missions in over 100 countries. Her Missionaries of Charity grew from twelve to thousands, serving the "poorest of the poor" in 450 centers worldwide. By the end of her life, Mother Theresa's co-workers numbered in the hundreds of thousands and it is estimated she had directly or indirectly touched and inspired hundreds of millions of the impoverished and underprivileged across the world.

Mother Teresa once said, "By blood, I am Albanian. By citizenship, an Indian. By faith, I am a Catholic nun. As to my calling, I belong to the world." Some of her more famous quotes exemplify the compassion, wisdom and love that defined her life:

"We think sometimes that poverty is only being hungry, naked and homeless. The poverty of being unwanted, unloved and uncared for is the greatest poverty. We must start in our own homes to remedy this kind of poverty."

"We need to find God, and he cannot be found in noise and restlessness. God is the friend of silence. See how nature - trees, flowers, grass- grows in silence; see the stars, the moon and the sun, how they move in silence... We need silence to be able to touch souls."

"Intense love does not measure; it just gives."

"If we have no peace, it is because we have forgotten that we belong to each other."

"We ourselves feel that what we are doing is just a drop in the ocean. But the ocean would be less because of that missing drop."

"I have found the paradox, that if you love until it hurts, there can be no more hurt, only more love."

"Love is a fruit in season at all times, and within reach of every hand. Anyone may gather it and no limit is set. Everyone can reach this love through meditation, spirit of prayer, and sacrifice, by an intense inner life."

"If you think well of others, you will also speak well of others and to others. From the abundance of the heart the mouth speaks. If your heart is full of love, you will speak of love."

"Don't look for big things, just do small things with great love….The smaller the thing, the greater must be our love."

"It is not how much you do, but how much Love you put into the doing that matters."

Chapter 10

The Lasting Capital of Knowledge; a Dynamic Model of Faith to Knowledge

Any discussion of your potentials is academic until such time as you gain enough experience applying correct assumptions to develop those potentials and come to a secure understanding that your potentials are real and they can be grown and developed. In other words, you must come to a personal knowledge of the truth and reality of your own potentials.

The subject of how any human can "know" something is the subject of immense philosophical debate. In fact, many great philosophers have come to the conclusion that you cannot actually "know" anything at all. However, the application of your potentials can be knowable, in fact must be knowable, within the realm of your current human experience. And again, if you operate under the six divine assumptions, such experience must be knowable in any form in which you would continue beyond this life.

Knowledge is the most valuable human capital. What we learn, and inevitably internalize and come to know, is the fabric of our existence. We can know facts and figures, such as the escape velocity of a vehicle needed to leave the gravitational pull of the earth. We can also know more ethereal concepts, such as the feeling of joy and pleasure when we first tasted premium ice cream.

Every shred of knowledge you accumulate throughout your life becomes a building block in the foundation of your character. The more "correct" or "useful" knowledge you accumulate, and subsequently act upon, the greater the trajectory and positive slope of your potentials. The more "negative" or "useless" or "trivial" (or worse detrimental) knowledge you accumulate the more neutral or negative the slope. All knowledge is not created equal when it comes to building and enhancing your potentials.

Accumulation of knowledge is a process. For some types of knowledge, particularly empirical knowledge, that process can be fairly simple. For instance, the formula for gravity can be ascertained by dropping a metal ball from various heights and recording the time it takes to reach the ground. You can repeat the experiment over and over and, without mitigating conditions, will get the exact same result again and again. By such experimentation you can come to a knowledge of certain conclusions. "If I drop a metal ball from 20 feet it will hit the ground in exactly so many seconds every time". We can even develop specific formula to describe such phenomena, such as $g=1/2\ at(2)$.

The process for intuitive knowledge is different however. Intuitive knowledge can be obtained through experimentation, but the results are not always precisely repeatable. While intuitive experimentation does not have the same reliability or possibility of measurement of empirical knowledge, it is a mistake to conclude that it is any less real…or any less valuable.

Intuitive knowledge is a process that requires the exercise of faith and the application of time and experience to come to a conclusion of that knowledge. The first step in any intuitive principle or potential is to start with an exercise of faith in that potential. And what exactly is that exercise of faith? It is simply that you believe that if you constantly apply a certain principle, it will begin to activate and develop the potential attached to that principle.

That faith must be exercised again and again. In time, you will start to see the results of constant exercise of faith. You will begin to receive intuitive insight, understanding. New perspectives will be opened, old perspectives may be broadened or modified. You will begin to broaden your understanding of that specific principle or potential. You may not always get the same result every time you exercise such faith, for in the world of the intuitive circumstances can vary widely. However, over time, a consistent pattern will emerge. With constant application and experience, that principle becomes an internalized and knowable fact. It is written upon your heart and mind as being real since it has yielded specific repeatable experiences that, as a whole, can be categorized as understanding or knowledge.

For example, if you were to adopt a puppy and raised that puppy with constant love, discipline and nurturing, you would learn over time that as the dog grows, it will respond consistently to your affections. If you behave a certain way each time, such as speaking kindly and scratching the dog's head with each positive behavior, over time you will have a sure knowledge that the dog has been conditioned and will react a certain way. But your knowledge extends deeper than just the understanding that certain conditioning yields certain results. It extends to the fact that a caring relationship towards the dog yields a caring relationship in return. The potential of love begets love. The experience gives you an undeniable understanding or knowledge of the fact that love is rewarded again with its own.

In this way, every intuitive potential and every piece of intuitive knowledge can be obtained and confirmed through experience. While the result are not equally as consistent as empirical tests due to the more complex circumstances and outcomes that can affect such intuitive experience, to you the reality is equally plausible. And even more, it is equally applicable when it comes to enjoying growth in your own views of the world. You learn what works and, in time, why it works.

These are the fruits of exercising such faith in your potential. Unlike empirical experiments, your intuitive potentials, skills and knowledge must be developed repeatedly and gradually over time. Your faith must never waiver as you begin to see at first a sprout, then a stem, then a broadening tree of understanding. In many cultures, such intuitive experience is considered the foundation of wisdom and, paired with the world of the empirical, completes or rounds out the library of understanding that defines human experience.

Epilogue: Händels' Messiah

It is a common occurrence around Christmas time to have groups gather to sing the famous composition "Handel's Messiah. This classic and timeless piece of music is a standout among great compositions of the age, both in it breadth and complexity. Georg Friedric Händel was born in Halle, Germany, into a religious, affluent household. His father, Georg Händel, a celebrated surgeon in northern Germany, wanted his son to study the law. But an acquaintance, the Duke of Weissenfels, heard the prodigy, then barely 11, playing the organ. The nobleman's recognition of the boy's genius likely influenced the doctor's decision to allow his son to become a musician. By 18, Handel had composed his first opera, Almira, initially performed in Hamburg in 1705. During the next five years, he was employed as a musician, composer and conductor at courts and churches in Rome, Florence, Naples and Venice, as well as in Germany, where the Elector of Hanover, the future King George I of England, was briefly his patron.

Händel was well accomplished at around 57 years of age when he composed the Messiah in August and September of 1741. But his experience in composition was unique in comparison to his other works. This particular piece, in his own words, was transferred from the intuitive, by a divine sense which he claimed to be beyond his own. Händel composed the entire 259 page original in three to four weeks. During this composition, he claimed unusual inspiration:

"Upon Händel's reading of God's word he was overcome in his spirit by its power and began to write "Messiah" in his study beginning, August 22nd, 1741. Several sources close to him record that Händel was so caught up in God's Spirit during the three weeks that it took him to write "Messiah", that he actually locked himself within his study, refusing food and writing music amid periods of crying and moaning in that same Spirit. Händel's servant testified in late summer, 1741: "He was praying, or he was weeping, or he was staring into eternity"
 Another servant's testimony is that at the end of this three week period Händel burst out of his study with tears in his eyes and the "Messiah" script in his hand declaring, that he had a great vision, and had seen God seated upon His throne: "I did think I did see all Heaven before me, and the great God Himself seated on His throne, with his Company of Angels."
Following the first London performance of Messiah, a patron congratulated Händel on the excellent "entertainment." "My lord, I should be sorry if I only entertained them," Händel humbly replied. "I wish to make them better."

Clearly Händel felt an unusual and intuitive inspiration in this particular work that has not been claimed in any other of his famous works. In his own history he proclaims how the gift of this music profoundly changed and healed his own life. The music stands to this day as a testimony of the power of the intuitive and inspirational. While we cannot measure or repeat the inspirational process that resulted in such a monumental work we can view and sing the fruits of that inspiration. And many continue do so each Christmas season.

Chapter 11

Every One can be a Genius…at something

If there is one misused nomenclature in modern culture it is the idea of genius. Albert Einstein is considered a genius. Thomas Edison was seen as a genius. And indeed they certainly were. And such accomplishment is always noteworthy, especially as it affects the broader outcomes of society. But genius does not just describe the realm of the extraordinary. It is possible to be one of the greatest physicists of all time. But in terms of the Salvation Equation, everyone can and should be a genius… at something.

What this implies is that within each one of us is something special. A propensity, an urge, a gift, a drive towards some aspect of our life and our internal motivation that leads us to be extraordinary in at least one area. For many of us, that "genius" can be multiplied into many specific applications or skills. But it is a fair assumption to believe that each one of us has something within us, perhaps something we were born with, which makes us special in our own particular way.

The key to growth and a positive ΔY within each of us is discovering, clearly identifying and then nurturing the growth of whatever genius we may be gifted with. You can be certain that if you are a living, breathing human being that you have the potential to be excellent, even transcendent at something. The question is what is your gift? Where does your personal genius abide? That, again, is a question for the ages. And when such innate ability is not immediately obvious, it may take time, years, even a significant portion of our lives, to see our internal genius realized.

The list of potentials outlined in the Salvation Equation is a good place to start. It may be a potential itself that describes your greatest personal abilities, or it may be a skill or application within that potential that naturally comes to the forefront in those times when you are able to reach for your best. One of the great keys to happiness and fulfillment is to be able to first recognize, then understand and then internalize and apply that specific genius within you.

Keep in mind that our application of the term genius does not necessarily mean you will discover the next great scientific, theological, social or political breakthrough. It does mean that somewhere inside of you is at least one thing that you can become so proficient at that others around you will consider you gifted at that particular skill or potential. And when that particular genius is shared and applied among others around you, it is a positive influence that advances the greater good of society as a whole.

If there was a blanket euphemism that could be applied to changing the world, the starting point might be to "find and unleash the genius within". It is the cumulative development and sharing of individual gifts that raises the bar with a community as a whole. It is a personal effort, but it is also a united team effort. The search for individual genius, along with the desire to use that genius to befit yourself and others positively, is a sure formula to change the face of the world itself. If an ideal structure were given to educational institutions, it would be a structure that worked under the assumption of elevating individual genius on a grand scale.

The search for personal meaning indeed starts with the questions "who am I" and "what am I good at". The next question that follows requires will, desire and the firm understanding of the need for positive ΔY, and that is "how may my gift benefit myself, my family, my friends and my community?"

Further, this is a question you should never be afraid of. It is a question that should generate excitement and the anticipation and faith that you will come to know, if you have not already, that a personal gift or gifts awaits discovery and development. In a sense, you can have a holiday of personal discovery as often as you want if you will simply accept that fact that you have personal value through the gift or gifts you may discover and share.

Think of what the world might be if everyone you knew saw themselves through this type of lens? What sort of changes would we see if everyone was concerned about nurturing their own positive gifts and the gifts of others? What sort of agendas would be important if our potentials, seen through the development of personal genius, were a priority in every activity we undertook?

While it requires imagination in our current paradigm of living, what efforts can you personally undertake to help change that paradigm? If you recognize gifts within yourself, can you recognize them in others? Can you see each individual you meet, no matter how attractive or seemingly lost, as someone with tremendous potential and a potential genius pertaining to at least one thing, whether small or great? Indeed, how could this understanding change your view of the world, your view of yourself, or of another?

Further, if there is a gift to be found within each of us, and we work under the seven divine assumptions, it follows that at least one of those gifts, if not many more, may be divine in nature? How would your perceptions change if you realized that every person you ever knew or would ever see has at least one divine gift or potential within them? Would such and understanding suggest a different perspective and perhaps a little kinder behavior and consideration, one to another? How different would our cultures be, our world be, if we each sought to activate our own divine gifts as well as seek those same standards in others. This is truly one way to save and change the world as we know it.

And inevitably the Salvation Equation does imply that we each have divine potential, thus divine gifts. We are indeed a genius at something, whether that genius can be temporally or eternally applied. The great mystery to our ultimate growth and development is to indeed choose to recognize the possibility of such gifts, and move forward with faith and determination to discover them and develop them, while encouraging others to do the same. What a world it could be if we all did exactly that!

<u>Epilogue - My friend Mark</u>

Just a few doors down lives a very special neighbor; my friend Mark. Mark has been our neighbor for nearly two decades. Mark is now well into his twenties but still requires complicated medical equipment, a wheelchair and someone to push it to be mobile. Mark was born under serious conditions, as his mother suffered a placental abruption. Mark cannot walk, or even stand. He cannot speak. He can only grunt and make a series of belabored cries. Mark's body is twisted and atrophied severely. Mark struggles every day just to eat, drink and hold on to life.

Mark's parents are kind, loving and patient and have given Mark every opportunity to live as normal a life as possible. He went to specialized schools and obtained the best education he could along with continual therapy. Behind his sparkling eyes, Mark is very perceptive and it is readily discernable that he understands the conversations and sociality that surrounds him. And Mark has a special gift.

Mark has the gift of perfect joy. He can discern the goodness, or lack thereof, in everyone he meets and can raise their sprits with a squeal and a smile. Mark is a genius at joyful compassion. He is a genius at both receiving and reflecting and communicating compassion and love. Mark seems to love nearly everyone he meets.

There are few people in this world that have a more difficult physical existence than Mark. In fact, it is a wonder Mark is still alive, as he defies the odds for his condition. Yet he seems inspired every day by his mission to communicate great joy at being alive and reflect the tremendous compassion he receives daily.

Without ever having uttered a word, Mark has become an inspiration to many. This is the fruit of true genius. It speaks to the importance, and the benefits, of each one of us finding and reflecting our unique genius within.

Chapter 12

We Are Ultimately Responsible for Unlocking Our Potentials and Maintaining Stewardship over them

In the final analysis, personal responsibility is the watchword of individual freedom of thought and action. As Victor Frankl, Abraham Maslow, Carl Rogers and others have pointed out in times past, no matter our circumstance we are each free to choose our own thoughts and actions. This freedom permeates every border, political or socioeconomic situation. While it is true that the consequences of those thoughts and actions may vary from country to country, from system to system, the fact that each individual can select their course of thought and desire is inarguable. And within freedom of thought is the freedom to realize our own potentials.

If our world is to truly achieve the highest levels of life and liberty, each one of us must choose within the confines of our own lives to be responsible for our thoughts and the actions that flow therefrom. The Salvation Equation suggests that the best way to achieve success in use of our freedoms of thought and action is to use that freedom to aspire to our highest and best potentials, even those potentials that suggest the divine nature within each of us. The Salvation Equation supports past theories that seek meaning and higher actualization in life and couples these with the notion that only through assuming certain divine principles can the highest actualization or potentials be achieved.

And that achievement begins with the simple process of individual choice. You have a responsibility, a stewardship, over your own decisions. No one else can make them for you. Even if you choose to surrender your freedom of action, you do so as a choice. You and you alone have the primary responsibility to develop uplifting and critical thought, thus determining what and who you will become. By choosing to recognize and pursue the potentials that lie within you, you are honoring that stewardship over self.

Everyone has an individual perception of how "fair" or "unfair" life is to them. Some choose to view this world as a karmic equation where good is returned for good and evil for evil. Others choose to see a random series of events that may or may not have any relationship as the course of a life unfolds. Some see a divine hand, or a type of "divine math" in everything. Regardless of the viewpoint, the one fact that remains is that you control your own thoughts and actions. And within those thoughts and actions resides the kernel of each and every potential you may ever attain. A famous theologian once posited "herein lies the freedom and potential condemnation of man; God will not force man to do any specific thing and the devil cannot". Even within the most turbulent maelstrom of good or evil, there still exists freedom of choice.

In short, the realization of your potentials is within your own hands. Neither chance nor divine intervention is the key to your growth, achievement and ultimate happiness. It rests within the little decisions you make each hour of each day. And the person who bears responsibility for those decisions is you. This innate understanding is the grand key to lasting upward potential. Embracing personal accountability is the quickest and most certain path to your highest potentials and true maturity.

Our modern culture often seeks to transfer the blame for circumstance onto others. And indeed there exist many circumstances and situations over which we may have little or no control. But what you do have control over is your reaction and determination to any circumstance, however bright or gloomy. The first question that might always be asked is "what can I do to make the situation more positive". If that answer takes into consideration your potential and the potential of others, it will undoubtedly be a more complete and insightful answer.

While one person may indeed make a profound impact upon themselves and others through personal stewardship, it remains for the great majority in any community or country to inevitably subscribe to the principles taught in the Salvation Equation in order to enjoy long term prosperity. Abrogating responsibility to any other paradigm or set of principles is proven by history to be unsustainable. While you must take pride in growing your own potentials, so must others around you for harmony to eventually prevail.

This fundamental progress of an individual or society in general boils down to the specific lens we choose through which to view our world. We can choose to subscribe to a limited view of current realities and project onto the limits of our own nature the restrictions, superstitions or fears of our current situation. Or, we may choose to adopt the lens of potential, especially divine potential, and see our lives and our world through the optimism of what it has the latent ability to become.

Fourth Dimensional Thought

As we begin to understand the benefits of assuming divine potential within each of us, the benefits of such perspective turn our thoughts upward, and our actions and preferences will naturally follow. As a majority of individuals choose to see the world from such an elevated perspective, the values and actions of a society begin to follow. Thus a changed world must begin with each elevated individual.

To begin to see the world in which we live as a function of a larger, divine progression is known as "fourth dimensional" thinking. This type of thought begins when the mundane thoughts of the day are replaced by the lens of a more enduring perspective. When we begin to see each thought and action as a small piece in a larger ongoing puzzle, a portrait of that larger puzzle starts to become clear over time. We begin to realize that our potentials are indeed important and that our time is well spent in discovering and nurturing them. When we act in the spirit of progression and accountability, we will tend to think and act in those terms as much or more than in other terms dictated by the fundamental needs of the day.

The natural result of utilizing the assumptions and pursuing the potentials described in the Salvation Equation is ultimately to begin to see and act through the perspective of fourth dimensional thought, a true "eternal perspective". You know you are making a transition into this broader paradigm when you begin to see the actions of your life and accomplishments in this world through the lens of the possibilities of divine assumptions, rather than seeing divine potential through the lens of the assumptions of this comparatively limited world.

Again, this is not to discount the place and function of the secular and scientific. It is simply to begin to recognize that the secular and scientific has its proper place, as does the intuitive and spiritual. To be able to think fourth dimensionally is to be able to give each framework its proper place and weight in forming a more complete picture of possible realities. Both the obvious every day realities and those realities that lie barely beyond the perception of daily experience. And indeed, fourth dimensional thought is earned through years of trial and error, experience with success and failure. It is a triumph of seeking wisdom as well as fact, of applying the true value of love into almost every situation and being uplifted and enlightened therefrom. The result is to be able to see everyday events through a lens of more divine, more eternal and more everlasting implications. And it is indeed such a perspective that has the innate power to change the world.

In man's longstanding search for meaning, in the struggle to place ourselves in the order of the universe, in the philosophical and religious pursuit of the ultimate status and destiny of man, the Salvation Equation sets forth the assumptions that can give each one of us an opportunity to form a perspective that can help us develop productive answers. Along with the opportunity to begin to achieve clarity on the proper direction of the personal journey that can lead to those answers.

And the fact remains, that if the assumptions of the divine are taken as true, and there exist potentials that remain intact and succeed the tenure of mortality, if your individuality indeed to continues on as the major religions and philosophies suggest, the final answers to life's greatest questions likely lie, at least in part, beyond our mortal experience. But that is not to say we cannot point ourselves in the proper direction to eventually obtain those answers. And that direction is dictated by the assumptions and potentials described in the Salvation Equation. If you can internalize these concepts, you can be assured that are at least headed in the right direction. After all, what would life be without a little mystery, and the requirement of faith that those mysteries must someday inevitably be solved?

In conclusion it is fair to say that without the assumption of nobility, purpose and divinity, our society would never have seen the progress it has. Without past generations balancing faith and reason, acting upon certain assumptions of the divine within each of us there would have been no renaissance, no age of enlightenment, no technological revolution and no information age. There would have been no flight, no exploration of space or missions to the moon. It was the great assumptions of potential, the determination of "what might be" that brings progress and civilization on an upward trend.

While the concepts of divinity within mankind can be turned and used as a tool of power or a hammer against one group or another, this is not the point or purpose of our potentials. Such use is, in fact, a usurpation of these uplifting principles. Any application of the divine within us that does not seek the positive slope of our potentials seeking to maximize the ΔY is a misuse of that principle. The Salvation Equation outlines the sets of assumptions and identifies specific potentials that can start you in a direction of progress. Progress upward in ability. Progress towards becoming a more complete and cognizant human being. Progress towards whatever your ultimate potential might be.

And in the final analysis, what better use of your time could there be than to look forward and upward, to seek the best that is within you? And if that best extends beyond the needs of the day and into the realm of the divine, how much more strident are the implications for who you are and who you may eventually become? If the intelligence of mankind has the potential to expand, and we must assume that it does, how powerful is the application of that intelligence to positive potentials over vast expanses of time? What would you eventually become if you increased in love, wisdom and knowledge according to those potentials not just within a lifetime, but beyond? What could an expanding human intelligence process over a period of millennia? The answer to that question likely holds the answers to the mysteries that have been sought by science and philosophy for so long. But science alone can never hold the key. Only with the application of both the empirical and the intuitive can a complete picture come into focus.

And so the understanding and application of the Salvation Equation can unlock your innate potentials. It can guide and direct you into a more complete picture of self. But remember, it is the journey that counts, for we are all, each and every one of us, engaged on that journey. It is simply a matter of direction, getting the divine compass working and being able to read and follow it well that counts.

May you be blessed to find great purpose in that journey!

Epilogue: Life More Abundantly

In the biblical history recorded in the New Testament, Jesus Christ is the central figure and the cornerstone of all modern Christianity. Despite all of the adoration, intellectual debate and skepticism surrounding the historical and mythical figure of Christ and his teachings, there are a few points that acolytes, casual observers and critics alike can agree on. First is the teaching of a principled and loving God and his precepts, whom he frequently referred to as "Father", a deliberate term. The second is a distinct reference to the reality of an afterlife. Christ stated succinctly: "I am come that they might have life, and that they might have it more abundantly" (John 10:10 KJV). The universal assumptions implied here are critical to the concepts of the Salvation Equation. The greatest abundance in our lives will stem from the sets of assumptions that ultimately guide, direct and refine the course of our lives.

A remarkable process occurs when we refuse to accept the seemingly obvious realities that surround us. New doors of perception open, new thoughts and understanding seem to distill upon our minds and our hearts. A more deeply layered and meaningful concept of the world around us takes shape. Our experiences deepen. In fact, this *is* an abundance, a greater fullness, a life slowly and deliberately instilled with more meaning. How is it possible not to attribute such a process to the spark of the divine nature within us? As we aspire to the highest possibilities we may imagine, we begin to perceive that such dreams may inevitably become reality.

The more aligned our assumptions with the deeper and more divine realities, the more those realities become clear and understood and the more empowered we are to live and grow by them. And unlocking such keys to our fullest lives is abundance indeed. Jesus Christ taught and lived these concepts in an exemplary way, even though his life's example demonstrates that elevating your assumptions above the accepted normality is not always smooth or comfortable. You have

the opportunity to live them also as your assumptions embrace and accept the divinity of your

own nature. Such a journey is never easy, but it is always worthwhile in every possible way.